THE SIMPLY EGGLESS COOKBOOK

ORIANA ROMERO

@MOMMYSHOMECOOKING

ACKNOWLEDGMENTS

I could not have written this book alone!

Thank You

To my readers on *Mommy's Home Cooking*, for your endless support and encouraging comments. The book would quite literally not exist without you and your enthusiasm for my recipes.

To my family, for supporting me in whatever I'm pursuing, especially my son-in-law Carlos who is always willing to lend a helping hand. You are amazing.

To my kids, Andrea, Matthew, and Victoria, and my grandson, Rapha. I love you to the moon and back again. You are my world.

To my husband, Victor, for your endearing support and endless encouragement, for all the emergency trips to the grocery store, and for being my biggest fan. I love you.

ISBN: 978-1-7360780-0-6 (Hardcover)
ISBN: 978-1-7360780-2-0 (Paperback)
ISBN: 978-1-7360780-1-3 (eBook)

Library of Congress Control Number: 2020925918

Names: Romero, Oriana, author

Title: The Simply Eggless Cookbook / Oriana Romero

Description: The ultimate guide for mastering egg-free cakes, cupcakes, cookies, brownies, and more…

Front Cover Design: Laura Nicholson – Pixel Me Designs

Back Cover and Interior Design: Raul Pina – Raul Pina Design

Lifestyle Photography: Luis Mateus & Marta Barata – Lounge Fotografia

Cake Decorator: Ana Pinto – Pó de Açúcar

First printing edition 2020
Printed in Spain

Oriana Romero Photography

12587 Fair Lakes Circle, #258

Fairfax, VA 22033, USA

www.mommyshomecooking.com

CONTENTS

WELCOME TO ORIANA'S EGGLESS KITCHEN

Hello! My name is Oriana, and I'm a wife, mom of three, recipe creator, writer, photographer, and the mastermind behind Mommy's Home Cooking, an eggless food blog. You can usually find me holed up in my home kitchen studio with flour on my clothes, splatters of butter in every direction, and a never-ending pile of dirty dishes.

And you know what? There is truly no place I'd rather be.

Why Eggless Recipes?

My youngest daughter, Victoria, was diagnosed with severe egg and nut allergies in 2013. Victoria was too young to realize what was going on, but I took it hard. Eggs had always been a huge part of our meals, and I was worried that our family's dynamic would completely change. No more pancakes, waffles, scrambled eggs, muffins… What would we even eat for breakfast?! Not to mention the challenge of special occasions like birthday parties, playdates, and school bake sales. Can you imagine a birthday party without a cake?

I've always believed egg allergies are one of the most difficult allergies to live with because eggs are hidden in so many different foods. When Victoria was diagnosed, I promised myself that I would never let her feel sidelined or limited by her condition. I refused to give up my lifelong passion for baking and cooking; I just had to find new ways to do it. To my delight, I discovered that with a little imagination and some perseverance, many dessert recipes could be made over into eggless treats without sacrificing flavor or texture.

And so my adventures of cooking and baking without eggs began, and my blog, Mommy's Home Cooking, evolved into a place where I could share my eggless recipes with the world.

Throughout the years, I have developed many delicious eggless recipes. I put all my love, passion, and attentiveness into every recipe I create. I care deeply about making every recipe the best it can be, which is why I test my recipes ten times over before I'm satisfied.

Baking without eggs can be frustrating at first, but don't worry! I've got you covered.

The Simply Eggless Cookbook is my dream come true.

Creating this cookbook has been the adventure of a lifetime. It is an extension of a dream I almost feel like I fell into, but it has enriched my life in countless ways and continues to do so.

This cookbook is a huge part of my heart, and I hope my recipes will prove as useful to your family as they have to mine. Whether you are a beginner or an expert baker, I know you'll love the recipes on these pages, and I truly hope they become a permanent part of your repertoire.

xo,

Oriana

BEFORE YOU START BAKING

Baking sweet, delicious treats can be a daunting task when you have to do it without eggs. Maybe you have never baked an eggless dessert before, or maybe you're a Suzy Homemaker. Either way, I have some basic guidelines to help you get great results every time you want to bake egg-free nibbles.

Read the Recipe before You Start!

Sounds pretty obvious, right? It's actually not uncommon for people to rush through the recipe and miss parts of it. Don't worry, I'm guilty of this too! Sometimes when I am in a rush, I don't take time to read the recipe. When you rush through a recipe like this, what happens? Do you usually end up with disappointing results? Have you ever left out an ingredient or gotten halfway through to find out you were missing something essential? Please, don't waste your time, effort, and money by hurrying through a recipe and skipping a step (or more).

Strictly Follow the Recipe

It can be tempting to substitute ingredients in a recipe based on what you have at home, but what are the results? They're often a disaster on a plate. I do not recommend doing this unless the recipe suggests suitable alternatives.

Measure Ingredients Correctly

There is no doubt about it. If you want to bake like a pro, you need to use a kitchen scale.

Baking is not very forgiving, and with no eggs, binding can get messed up if the ingredient ratio is not perfect. To put it plainly, the difference between successful and failed eggless baking can lie in adding a little too much or too little of any one ingredient.

Most American kitchens are equipped to measure ingredients by volume with measuring cups and measuring spoons, but I highly recommend using a kitchen scale. A scale is not a big investment, but it will fundamentally change your baking results.

Use Ingredients at Room Temperature

This simple baking tip is often overlooked. Bakers take it lightly and pour ingredients right out of their refrigerators. Well, if you want a better texture and light, puffy bites, quit it! The results will pleasantly surprise you.

There are scientific reasons behind this advice. When butter and milk are at room temperature, they emulsify to capture air. Then the trapped air bubbles grow with the heat in the oven, achieving a bakery-worthy, fluffy texture in your cakes and cupcakes.

When I call for "softened" butter, it means the stick of butter will easily bend without breaking and will give slightly when pressed. To soften butter, let the refrigerated butter sit at room temperature for about 30 minutes; cut the butter into pieces to speed up the process. If you are short on time, you can place the cold butter in a resealable plastic bag and pound it with a rolling pin until it reaches the desired temperature (65°–67°F / 18°–20°C).

Don't Overbeat the Batter!

What happens when you overmix the batter, particularly when it is eggless?

Overbeating gives your cake and cupcakes a tough texture because all the air gets deflated. By overmixing the batter, you are also overdeveloping the gluten.

Mix just until you've evenly distributed the ingredients throughout the batter. Use a plastic spatula to scrape the sides of the bowl, and don't forget to scrape the bottom of the bowl for any pockets of flour or other ingredients.

Don't Open the Oven until the Baked Good Has Set

It can be super-tempting to open the oven every few minutes to check on your cake. For the sake of baking a perfectly puffy cake, don't—at least not during the first two-thirds of the total baking time.

Each time you open the oven door, you let out some heat, causing the temperature inside to drop. This will also lead the rising cake to sink because the cake's interior will not get time to rise and set properly.

So what's the takeaway idea?

Leave the oven closed until the minimum time stated in the recipe.

If you have to check on your cake before it's ready, do so by pulling the rack out instead of removing the whole cake from the oven.

Know Your Oven

Every oven is different. Unless you have a new or regularly calibrated oven, its temperature is likely inaccurate. Because of this, your baking time can vary, and an inaccurate oven can ruin your baked goods if you don't adjust accordingly.

Here are some tips to help avoid oven-temp issues:

- Preheat the oven at least 15 minutes before you get started to give it plenty of time to reach the ideal recipe temperature.

- Place an oven thermometer in your oven so you can read the accurate inside temperature in real time.

EGGLESS BAKING KEY INGREDIENTS

Apple Cider Vinegar

As an acidic ingredient, apple cider vinegar tenderizes, and combined with baking powder and soda, it helps your baked goods rise. Apple cider vinegar can be substituted for white vinegar or fresh lemon juice.

Applesauce

All the recipes in this book that call for applesauce were tested with unsweetened applesauce. To make applesauce at home, peel, core, and slice 2 to 3 apples. Place the apples in a large microwave-safe bowl. Add 1 tablespoon of water and a pinch of cinnamon; stir to combine. Cover with heavy microwave-safe plastic wrap (leave a little opening on one side to allow steam to escape). Microwave on high power for 2 to 3 minutes, or until fork-tender. Using a large fork, a small food processor, or a blender, mash the apples until smooth. Bring to room temperature and then refrigerate for up to two days.

Aquafaba

Aquafaba is the liquid that we usually discard from a can of beans. This slimy liquid emulates the unmistakably fluffy texture of whipped egg whites. I mostly use the aquafaba from canned chickpeas.

Scan with your phone to learn how to make aquafaba

Brown Sugar

Brown sugar is granulated sugar that has been combined with molasses to add a deep caramel flavor. Dark brown sugar has more molasses than light brown sugar. If either can be used, I simply call for brown sugar.

Butter

Most recipes in this book use unsalted butter. That is because I like to control the amount of salt I add to my recipes. Also, salted butter contains more water than unsalted butter, and the extra water can affect gluten development. If you substitute unsalted butter for salted butter, reduce the salt called for in the recipe by half.

When I call for softened butter, it means the stick of butter will easily bend without breaking and will give slightly when pressed.

I do not recommend substituting oil for butter. Butter adds a surprising amount of flavor to cakes and cupcakes, particularly vanilla or plain ones. Most of my recipes are made by the creaming method—beating butter and sugar together—which helps to incorporate air into the batter to make it fluffy. If you use oil, the cake will be flatter and denser.

Buttermilk

Buttermilk is mostly used for better texture and extra fluffiness. If you don't have buttermilk handy, you can make your own homemade substitute by adding a tablespoon of vinegar to a cup of milk.

Chocolate

The type and brand of chocolate you use can make a big difference. Milk, semisweet, and bittersweet (dark) chocolate contain different amounts of cacao; the higher the cacao percentage, the more intense the chocolate flavor. In most of my recipes, I like to use semisweet chocolate with 50 to 60 percent cacao. Of course, you can use the chocolate that best suits your personal taste.

Cocoa

All recipes in this book use unsweetened natural cocoa powder, which is more acidic and reacts with baking soda, allowing your baked goods to rise. If you live in the US, the cocoa powder you most often see in the baking aisle, like Hershey's or Ghirardelli, is natural. Flavor varies by brand, but you can always find me using either of these two. Try to avoid Dutched cocoa for these recipes.

Cream Cheese

I use cream cheese as a baking ingredient in some of my eggless recipes to add richness. I mainly use plain, full-fat cream cheese.

Flour

Flour might be the most important ingredient for baking. It gives baked goods structure, crumb, and texture, which is super important, especially in eggless desserts. The flour I use in this book is all-purpose flour, which has a moderate protein content of 10 to 11.7 percent, depending on the brand.

If you are not in the US, check the protein content of the flour you are using. Use a flour with 8 to 10 percent protein content for better results. Higher-protein-content flour may result in a drier and denser baked good.

Food Coloring

Gel food coloring has a higher concentration of color than liquid coloring, which means you can use less to reach the color you want. This also means that you are not adding extra liquid to the recipe. I always use AmeriColor gel food coloring.

Heavy Cream

When a recipe calls for heavy cream, use a cream with around 35 percent fat content. In the US and Canada, that means heavy whipping cream. In the UK and Australia, double cream will work fine. Keep cream chilled for better results when whipping. A dairy-free alternative for heavy cream is full-fat canned coconut milk (make sure to shake it before opening).

Instant Espresso Powder

Many of my chocolate recipes call for instant espresso powder mixed with hot water to enhance the chocolate flavor. You won't taste the coffee, but if you prefer not to use coffee, add the hot water on its own.

Milk

I often use whole milk in my recipes; the fat in the whole milk tenderizes the crumb and can weaken gluten. You can also use 2 percent or 1 percent milk if that is what you have handy. If you have a dairy restriction, cow's milk can be replaced with soy milk or another plant-based milk in most recipes.

Oil

Using an oil with a neutral flavor is key. Whenever a recipe calls for oil, use vegetable, canola, or soy oil. I do not recommend switching between oil and butter in my recipes.

Regular Plain Yogurt and/or Sour Cream

Yogurt and sour cream, both acidic, produce similar results to buttermilk but make your baked goods even more tender. Yogurt and sour cream may be used interchangeably in my recipes. I recommend using the full-fat versions.

Salt

I prefer to use kosher or sea salt for baking. They're iodine-free, which makes them better tasting. You can also use iodine-free table salt. I recommend picking one brand and sticking with it for consistency. Flaked sea salt is great for sprinkling on top of baked goods.

Sugar

I mainly use granulated sugar, which is also known in other parts of the world as caster or superfine sugar. It's your regular, everyday, white sugar. The other sugar called for in this book is confectioners' sugar, also known as powdered sugar, icing sugar, or 10x sugar.

Vanilla

Use pure vanilla extract for better taste. A couple of recipes in this book call for vanilla beans, which impart a deeper flavor than extract.

KITCHEN EQUIPMENT AND TOOL ESSENTIALS

There are certain pieces of equipment that make baking easier and more accurate. Here's what you'll need to put these eggless sweet treats on your table:

- 12-count cupcake/muffin pan
- 6-count jumbo muffin pan
- Baking sheets
- Bundt pan
- Cake cutter or leveler
- Cake decorating stand turntable
- Chef's knife
- Cookie cutters
- Cookie scoop (#40 – holds 1.5 tablespoons of dough)
- Cooling rack
- Digital scale
- Loaf pan
- Mixing bowls
- Offset spatula
- Oven thermometer
- Parchment paper
- Pastry brush
- Piping set
- Rasp-style grater
- Rectangular baking pan
- Rolling pin
- Round cake pans (6-, 7-, and 8-inch)
- Rubber spatulas
- Ruler
- Serrated knife
- Sifter
- Springform pan
- Square baking pan
- Stand mixer or electric handheld mixer
- Whisk

Visit my online shop to find my kitchen favorites and key eggless ingredients!

Scan with your phone to
see my favorites

CAKES

EGGLESS CLASSIC YELLOW BIRTHDAY CAKE

When you think of birthday cake, the first thing that comes to mind is a delicious yellow cake smothered in chocolate frosting. This eggless version of the classic is the perfect birthday cake for kids and adults. It's two layers of fluffy yellow cake filled and decorated with chocolate buttercream and tons of sprinkles—what's not to love?

Makes one 2-layer, 8-inch (20-cm) cake, serves 10 to 12

For the Eggless Yellow Cake

4 cups (560 g) all-purpose flour

1 tablespoon + 2 teaspoons (20 g) baking powder

1/2 teaspoon (3 g) baking soda

1/2 teaspoon (2 g) salt

2 cups (480 ml) milk

2 tablespoons (30 ml) apple cider vinegar

1 cup (230 g) unsalted butter, softened

2 cups (400 g) granulated sugar

1/4 cup (60 g) plain regular yogurt

2 teaspoons (10 ml) pure vanilla extract

Generous pinch of ground turmeric for color

To Assemble and Decorate

1 batch American Chocolate Buttercream (page 145)

1 cup (190 g) sprinkles

Make the Eggless Yellow Cake

Preheat the oven to 350ºF (180ºC). Line two 8-inch (20-cm) round cake pans with parchment paper. Lightly grease with baking spray with flour.

Sift the flour, baking powder, baking soda, and salt together into a large bowl.

In a mixing bowl or liquid measuring cup, combine the milk and vinegar. Let the mixture rest for 5 to 8 minutes, until thickened and curdled.

Using an electric hand mixer or a stand mixer, beat the butter on medium-high speed until creamy, 3 to 4 minutes. Add the sugar and beat on high speed for 4 minutes, until creamed and pale, scraping down the sides and up the bottom of the bowl with a rubber spatula as needed. Then add the yogurt, vanilla, and turmeric; continue beating to combine, about 1 minute.

Turn the mixer to low and add the flour mixture in three batches, alternating with the milk mixture, beginning and ending with the flour mixture. Beat until just combined, 30 to 45 seconds. Do not overmix.

Evenly divide the batter between the prepared pans.

Bake for 23 to 28 minutes, or until a toothpick inserted in the center comes out clean. Let the cakes cool in their pans on wire racks for 10 minutes, and then remove from the pans. Allow the cakes to cool completely, right-side up, on wire racks before removing the parchment paper.

Unfrosted cake layers can be stored at room temperature for up to 2 days or frozen for up to a month; defrost at room temperature before frosting and serving. Take into consideration that the cakes will lose some of their fluffiness if refrigerated or frozen.

Assemble and Decorate

Level the tops of the cakes with a cake cutter or a long, serrated knife as needed.
Line the edges of a cake platter with four strips of parchment paper to keep the platter clean.

Place the first cake layer on the platter. Spread 1 cup of buttercream evenly over the top. Top with the second cake layer, pressing lightly to adhere. Then spread 1-1/2 cups buttercream evenly over the top and sides of the cake. You can smooth the cake's top and sides with the edge of an offset spatula to smooth out any bumps.

Place the remaining buttercream in a piping bag fitted with your favorite piping tip. Add as many swirls on the top of the cake as you like. Gently press sprinkles onto the cake's sides, and then top with more sprinkles. Remove the parchment paper strips and serve. The frosted cake can be stored at room temperature for up to 2 days or in the refrigerator for up to 5 days.

Scan with your phone to learn **How to Stack A Layer Cake**

> **ORIANA'S NOTES:**
>
> If you don't have turmeric, you can add a couple drops of yellow paste food coloring to the batter.

EGGLESS OLD-FASHIONED CHOCOLATE LAYER CAKE

Everyone needs a great chocolate cake recipe! This Old-Fashioned Eggless Chocolate Layer Cake has a tender, airy, open crumb that you are going to love. It's soft and velvety, deeply flavorful and rich, and extra moist. And as if that were not enough, it's covered with a decadent eggless Swiss meringue buttercream and ganache! This extra-chocolatey cake is super easy to make; you don't even need an electric mixer.

Makes one 3-layer, 6-inch (15-cm) cake, serves 10 to 12

For the Eggless Chocolate Layer Cake

2 cups (400 g) granulated sugar

1-1/2 cups (360 ml) buttermilk

1/2 cup (115 g) unsalted butter, melted

1/2 cup (120 ml) vegetable or canola oil

1/2 cup (120 g) sour cream

2 teaspoons (10 ml) pure vanilla extract

2 tablespoons (30 ml) hot water (optional)

2 teaspoons (2 g) instant espresso powder (optional)

2-1/2 cups (350 g) all-purpose flour

3/4 cup (90 g) unsweetened natural cocoa powder

1 tablespoon + 1 teaspoon (16 g) baking powder

1/2 teaspoon (3 g) baking soda

1/2 teaspoon (2 g) salt

To Assemble and Decorate

1 medium batch Eggless Chocolate Swiss Meringue Buttercream (page 153)

1 batch Chocolate Ganache (page 165)

Make the Eggless Chocolate Layer Cake

Preheat the oven to 350ºF (180ºC). Line three 6-inch (15-cm) round cake pans with parchment paper. Lightly grease with baking spray with flour.

Combine the sugar, buttermilk, melted butter, oil, sour cream, and vanilla extract in a large bowl and whisk together.

In a small bowl, combine the hot water and instant espresso powder, if using. Add to the butter mixture; mix to combine.

Add the flour, cocoa powder, baking powder, baking soda, and salt; stir until just combined.

Evenly divide the batter among the prepared pans.

Bake for 25 to 35 minutes, or until a toothpick inserted in the center comes out clean. Let the cakes cool in their pans on wire racks for 10 minutes, and then remove them from the pans. Allow the cakes to cool completely, right-side up, on wire racks before removing the parchment paper.

Unfrosted cake layers can be stored at room temperature for up to 2 days or frozen for up to a month; defrost at room temperature before frosting and serving. Take into consideration that the cakes will lose some of their fluffiness if refrigerated or frozen.

Assemble and Decorate

Level the tops of the cakes with a cake cutter or a long, serrated knife as needed.
Line the edges of a cake platter with four strips of parchment paper to keep the platter clean.

Place the first cake layer on the platter. Spread 1 cup of buttercream evenly over the top. Top with the second cake layer and press lightly to adhere. Repeat to add the third layer, and then spread about 1-1/2 cups buttercream evenly over the top and sides of the cake. You can smooth the cake's top and sides with the edge of an offset spatula to smooth out any bumps.

Add the ganache drip. Use a spoon to add the ganache around the top edge of the cake and gently push it over the edge so it falls, creating a drip. Continue adding drips around the outer edge until you've gone all the way around. Then fill in the center, pouring the remaining ganache onto the top of the cake and using your offset spatula to spread it evenly. Refrigerate the cake for 15 minutes to set the drip.

Place the remaining buttercream in a piping bag fitted with your favorite piping tip. Add as many swirls on the top of the cake as you like. Remove the parchment paper strips and serve. The frosted cake can be stored at room temperature for up to 2 days or in the refrigerator for up to 5 days.

Scan with your phone for my **Eggless Chocolate Sheet Cake Recipe**

EGGLESS BANANA LAYER CAKE

If you love banana bread, you are going to love this triple-layered, moist, and flavorful banana cake filled and topped with Salted Caramel Buttercream. It's hard to beat the combination of banana and salted caramel. I guarantee that everyone will love this cake—it's the best eggless banana cake, hands down.

Makes one 3-layer, 6-inch (15-cm) cake, serves 10 to 12

For the Eggless Banana Cake

3 cups (420 g) all-purpose flour

1 tablespoon (12 g) baking powder

1 teaspoon (6 g) baking soda

1 teaspoon (2 g) ground cinnamon

1/2 teaspoon (2 g) salt

1 cup (240 ml) milk

1 tablespoon (15 ml) apple cider vinegar

1 cup (230 g) unsalted butter, softened

1 cup (200 g) granulated sugar

1/2 cup (100 g) brown sugar

3 ripe bananas, mashed (about 1-1/2 cups / 240 g)

1/2 cup (120 g) regular plain yogurt

2 teaspoons (10 ml) pure vanilla extract

To Assemble and Decorate

1 batch Salted Caramel Buttercream (page 156)

1 batch Salted Caramel (page 166)

Biscoff cookies (optional)

Scan with your phone for my **Eggless Classic Banana Bread Recipe**

ORIANA'S NOTES:

If you find that the tops of the cakes are browning too quickly in the oven, loosely cover them with aluminum foil. The caramel drip won't stay in place like a traditional ganache, so add it at the last minute before serving.

Make the Eggless Banana Cake

Preheat the oven to 350ºF (180ºC). Line three 6-inch (15-cm) round cake pans with parchment paper. Lightly grease with baking spray with flour.

Sift the flour, baking powder, baking soda, cinnamon, and salt together into a large bowl.

In a mixing bowl or liquid measuring cup, combine the milk and vinegar. Let the mixture rest for 5 to 8 minutes, until thickened and curdled.

Using an electric hand mixer or a stand mixer, beat the butter on medium-high speed until creamy, 3 to 4 minutes. Add the sugars and beat on high speed for 4 minutes until creamed and smooth, scraping down the sides and up the bottom of the bowl with a rubber spatula as needed. Then add the mashed bananas, yogurt, and vanilla; continue beating to combine, about 1 minute.

Turn the mixer to low and add the flour mixture in three batches, alternating with the milk mixture, beginning and ending with the flour mixture. Beat until just combined, 30 to 45 seconds. Do not overmix.

Evenly divide the batter among the prepared pans.

Bake for 40 to 50 minutes, or until a toothpick inserted in the center comes out clean. Let the cakes cool in their pans on wire racks for 10 minutes, and then remove from the pans. Allow the cakes to cool completely, right-side up, on wire racks before removing the parchment paper.

Unfrosted cake layers can be stored at room temperature for up to 2 days or frozen for up to a month; defrost at room temperature before frosting and serving. Take into consideration that the cakes will lose some of their fluffiness if refrigerated or frozen.

Assemble and Decorate

Level the tops of the cakes with a cake cutter or a long, serrated knife as needed.

Line the edges of a cake platter with four strips of parchment paper to keep the platter clean.

Place the first cake layer on the platter. Spread 1 cup of buttercream evenly over the top and drizzle with 1/4 cup salted caramel. Top with the second cake layer, pressing lightly to adhere. Repeat to add the third layer, and then spread about 1-1/2 cups buttercream evenly over the top and sides of the cake. You can smooth the cake's top and sides with the edge of an offset spatula to smooth out any bumps.

Add a layer of caramel onto the top of the cake and smooth. You can add additional drips of caramel onto the side of the cake, if desired.

Place the remaining buttercream in a piping bag fitted with your favorite piping tip. Pipe on a decorative buttercream rim. Top the cake with crushed Biscoff cookies, if desired. Remove the parchment paper and serve. The frosted cake can be stored at room temperature for up to 1 day or in the refrigerator for up to 5 days.

EGGLESS STRAWBERRY CREAM CAKE

This Eggless Strawberry Cream Cake with Whipped Cream Frosting was one of the first recipes I created for this book. In fact, everyone loved it so much that it made it to the cover. Packed with fresh strawberries, whipped cream, and vanilla, it's a totally heavenly dessert recipe that is a favorite anytime of the year and sure to impress!

Makes one 3-layer, 7-inch (18-cm) cake, serves 10 to 12

For the Eggless Vanilla Cake

4 cups (560 g) all-purpose flour

1 tablespoon + 2 teaspoons (20 g) baking powder

1/2 teaspoon (3 g) baking soda

1/2 teaspoon (2 g) salt

2 cups (480 ml) milk

2 tablespoons (30 ml) apple cider vinegar

1 cup (230 g) unsalted butter, softened

2 cups (400 g) granulated sugar

1/4 cup (60 g) plain regular yogurt

2 teaspoons (10 ml) pure vanilla extract

For the Strawberry Filling

1 pound (454 g) fresh strawberries, hulled and cut into small pieces (about 3 cups)

3 tablespoons (36 g) granulated sugar

To Assemble and Decorate

1 batch Whipped Cream Frosting (page 161)

Fresh strawberries to taste (optional)

Make the Eggless Vanilla Cake

Preheat the oven to 350°F (180°C). Line three 7-inch (18-cm) round cake pans with parchment paper. Lightly grease with baking spray with flour.

Sift the flour, baking powder, baking soda, and salt together into a large bowl.

In a mixing bowl or liquid measuring cup, combine the milk and vinegar. Let the mixture rest for 5 to 8 minutes, until thickened and curdled.

Using an electric hand mixer or a stand mixer, beat the butter on medium-high speed until creamy, 3 to 4 minutes. Add the sugar and beat on high speed for 4 minutes until creamed and pale, scraping down the sides and up the bottom of the bowl with a rubber spatula as needed. Then add the yogurt and vanilla; continue beating to combine, about 1 minute.

Turn the mixer to low and add the flour mixture in three batches, alternating with the milk mixture, beginning and ending with the flour mixture. Beat until just combined, 30 to 45 seconds. Do not overmix.

Evenly divide the batter among the prepared pans.

Bake for 23 to 28 minutes, or until a toothpick inserted in the center comes out clean. Let the cakes cool in their pans on wire racks for 10 minutes, and then remove from the pans. Allow the cakes to cool completely, right-side up, on wire racks before removing the parchment paper.

Unfrosted cake layers can be stored at room temperature for up to 2 days or frozen for up to a month; defrost at room temperature before frosting and serving. Take into consideration that the cakes will lose some of their fluffiness if refrigerated or frozen.

Make the Strawberry Filling

Toss the chopped strawberries and sugar together in a bowl and let sit for 1 hour, stirring occasionally. Drain the berries in a fine-mesh strainer set over a bowl and reserve the juice.

Assemble and Decorate

Level the tops of the cakes with a cake cutter or a long, serrated knife as needed.

Line the edges of a cake platter with four strips of parchment paper to keep the platter clean.

Mix the drained strawberries with 2 cups of the whipped cream frosting.

Place the first cake layer on the platter. Brush the cake with 2–3 tablespoons of the reserved strawberry juice. Spread 1 cup of whipped cream frosting evenly over the top. Top with half of the strawberry filling. Top with the second cake layer, pressing lightly to adhere. Repeat to add the third layer, and then spread the remaining whipped cream frosting evenly over the top and sides of the cake. You can smooth the cake's top and sides with the edge of an offset spatula to smooth out any bumps.

Garnish with fresh strawberries, if desired. Remove the parchment paper strips and serve. The frosted cake can be stored in the refrigerator for up to 4 hours.

ORIANA'S NOTES:

You can substitute strawberries with raspberries or blackberries if you like.

EGGLESS CARROT LAYER CAKE

The best eggless carrot cake you'll ever make, this incredibly moist, eggless cake is infused with spices, loaded with carrots, frosted with a cream cheese frosting, and garnished with walnuts. It comes together easily and is pretty enough for company yet easy enough for a family dinner!

Makes one 2-layer, 8-inch (20-cm) cake, serves 10 to 12

For the Eggless Carrot Cake

3 cups (420 g) all-purpose flour

2-1/4 cups (360 g) granulated sugar

1 tablespoon + 1 teaspoon (16 g) baking powder

1-1/2 (9 g) teaspoons baking soda

2 teaspoons (4 g) ground cinnamon

1/2 teaspoon (1 g) ground nutmeg

1/4 teaspoon (0.5 g) ground cloves

1/2 teaspoon (2 g) salt

1 cup + 2 tablespoons (270 ml) buttermilk

1 cup (240 ml) vegetable oil

1/2 cup (130 g) unsweetened applesauce

2 teaspoons (10 ml) pure vanilla extract

3 cups (380 g) shredded carrots

To Assemble and Decorate

2 batches Cream Cheese Frosting (page 161)

1 cup (120 g) chopped walnuts

Make the Eggless Carrot Cake

Preheat the oven to 350ºF (180ºC). Line two 8-inch (20-cm) round cake pans with parchment paper. Lightly grease with baking spray with flour.

In a large bowl, whisk together the flour, sugar, baking powder, baking soda, cinnamon, nutmeg, cloves, and salt.

Add the buttermilk, oil, applesauce, and vanilla; stir until just combined. Fold in the shredded carrots.

Evenly divide the batter between the prepared pans.

Bake for 30 to 40 minutes, or until a toothpick inserted in the center comes out clean. Let the cakes cool in their pans on wire racks for 10 minutes, and then remove from the pans. Allow the cakes to cool completely, right-side up, on wire racks before removing the parchment paper.

Unfrosted cake layers can be stored at room temperature for up to 2 days or frozen for up to a month; defrost at room temperature before frosting and serving. Take into consideration that the cakes will lose some of their fluffiness if refrigerated or frozen.

Assemble and Decorate

Level the tops of the cakes with a cake cutter or a long, serrated knife as needed.
Line the edges of a cake platter with four strips of parchment paper to keep the platter clean.

Place the first cake layer on the platter. Spread 1 cup of frosting evenly over the top. Top with the second cake layer, pressing lightly to adhere. Cover the top and sides of the cake evenly with about 2 cups frosting. You can smooth the cake's top and sides with the edge of an offset spatula to smooth out any bumps.

Place the remaining frosting in a piping bag fitted with your favorite piping tip. Add as many swirls on the top of the cake as you like. Gently press chopped walnuts onto the cake's sides. Remove the parchment paper and serve. The frosted cake can be stored at room temperature for up to 1 day or in the refrigerator for up to 5 days.

Scan with your phone to learn **how to make buttermilk substitute at home**

ORIANA'S NOTES:

Shred carrots on the large holes of a box grater or in a food processor fitted with the shredding disk.

EGGLESS RED VELVET SHEET CAKE

Red velvet is my son's favorite cake! This Eggless Red Velvet Sheet Cake is moist, rich, and amazingly tasty! Sometimes you just don't feel like layering cakes, so a sheet cake is the way to go—a single layer of vibrant red sponge cake with fluffy cream cheese frosting. I promise you will not miss the eggs. Use this cake recipe as a birthday sheet cake or for anytime you crave a simple, classic dessert.

Makes one 9 x 13 inch (24 x 35 cm) cake, serves 12 to 16

For the Eggless Red Velvet Cake

3 cups (420 g) all-purpose flour

1 tablespoon + 1 teaspoon (16 g) baking powder

1 teaspoon (6 g) baking soda

2 tablespoons (15 g) unsweetened cocoa powder

1/2 teaspoon (2 g) salt

1/2 cup (115 g) unsalted butter, softened

2 cups (400 g) granulated sugar

1 cup (240 ml) vegetable oil

1/2 cup (120 g) regular plain yogurt

2 teaspoons (10 ml) pure vanilla extract

1 teaspoon (5 ml) apple cider vinegar

1 tablespoon (15 ml) paste or gel red food coloring

1 cup (240 ml) buttermilk

To Assemble and Decorate

1 batch Cream Cheese Frosting (page 161)

Make the Eggless Red Velvet Cake

Preheat the oven to 350ºF (180ºC). Line a 9 x 13 inch (24 x 35 cm) baking pan with parchment paper. Lightly grease with baking spray with flour.

Sift the flour, baking powder, baking soda, cocoa powder, and salt together into a large bowl.

Using an electric hand mixer or a stand mixer, beat the butter on medium-high speed until creamy, 3 to 4 minutes. Add the sugar and beat on high speed for 4 minutes, until creamed and pale, scraping down the sides and up the bottom of the bowl with a rubber spatula as needed. Then add the oil, yogurt, vanilla, vinegar, and food coloring; continue beating until well combined, about 2 minutes.

Turn the mixer to low and add the flour mixture in three batches, alternating with the buttermilk, beginning and ending with the flour mixture. Beat until just combined, 30 to 45 seconds. Do not overmix.

Pour the batter into the prepared pan.

Bake for 45 to 55 minutes, or until a toothpick inserted in the center comes out clean. Let the cake cool in the pan on a wire rack for 20 minutes, and then remove from the pan. Allow the cake to cool completely, right-side up, on a wire rack before removing the parchment paper.

The unfrosted cake can be stored at room temperature for up to 2 days or frozen for up to a month; defrost at room temperature before frosting and serving. Take into consideration that the cake will lose some of its fluffiness if refrigerated or frozen.

Assemble and Decorate

Frost the cooled cake with the cream cheese frosting and smooth the top with an offset spatula. Slice and serve. The frosted cake can be stored at room temperature for up to 1 day or in the refrigerator for up to 5 days.

Scan with your phone for my **Eggless Red Velvet Cupcakes Recipe**

ORIANA'S NOTES:

You can also use a 12 x 17 inch (29 x 42 cm) half-sheet pan to make this recipe.

EGGLESS RASPBERRY VANILLA BEAN LAYER CAKE

This classic layer cake pairs a moist, eggless vanilla bean cake with a sweet raspberry filling. The entire cake is frosted with our absolute favorite—a Vanilla Swiss Meringue Buttercream that's so good you'll want to spread it on everything. You can swap out the raspberry jam for strawberry, blackberry, blueberry, grape, or any other of your family's favorite flavors.

Makes one 3-layer, 6-inch (15-cm) cake, serves 10 to 12

For the Eggless Vanilla Bean Cake

4 cups (560 g) all-purpose flour

1 tablespoon + 2 teaspoons (20 g) baking powder

1/2 teaspoon (3 g) baking soda

1/2 teaspoon (2 g) salt

2 cups (480 ml) milk

2 tablespoons (30 ml) apple cider vinegar

1 cup (230 g) unsalted butter, softened

2 cups (400 g) granulated sugar

2 vanilla beans

1/4 cup (60 g) plain regular yogurt

2 teaspoons (10 ml) pure vanilla extract

To Assemble and Decorate

1 medium batch Eggless Vanilla Swiss Meringue Buttercream (page 152)

1/3 cup (80 g) raspberry jam

10–12 fresh raspberries

ORIANA'S NOTES:

Ombre Decoration: After layering the cake, divide the remaining buttercream into three equal amounts to create the ombre effect shown here. Add paste food coloring to each batch to create three shades of the same color frosting. Spread the darkest-colored buttercream over the bottom third of the sides of the cake, the medium-colored buttercream over the middle third, and the lightest-colored buttercream over the top third and the top of the cake.

While spinning the cake turntable, run a small spatula from the bottom to the top of the cake's side to blend the frosting colors. Then run the spatula over the top of the cake, working from the outside in, to create a spiral.

Make the Eggless Vanilla Bean Cake

Preheat the oven to 350ºF (180ºC). Line three 6-inch (15-cm) round cake pans with parchment paper. Lightly grease with baking spray with flour.

Sift the flour, baking powder, baking soda, and salt together into a large bowl.

In a mixing bowl or liquid measuring cup, combine the milk and vinegar. Let the mixture rest for 5 to 8 minutes, until thickened and curdled.

Using an electric hand mixer or a stand mixer, beat the butter on medium-high speed until creamy, 3 to 4 minutes. Add the sugar and beat on high speed for 4 minutes, until creamed and pale, scraping down the sides and up the bottom of the bowl with a rubber spatula as needed. Split the vanilla beans and scrape the seeds into the creamed mixture; discard the beans. Add the yogurt and vanilla and continue beating to combine, about 1 minute.

Turn the mixer to low and add the flour mixture in three batches, alternating with the milk mixture, beginning and ending with the flour mixture. Beat until just combined, 30 to 45 seconds. Do not overmix.

Evenly divide the batter among the prepared pans.

Bake for 23 to 28 minutes, or until a toothpick inserted in the center comes out clean. Let the cakes cool in their pans on wire racks for 10 minutes, and then remove from the pans. Allow the cakes to cool completely, right-side up, on wire racks before removing the parchment paper.

Unfrosted cake layers can be stored at room temperature for up to 2 days or frozen for up to a month; defrost at room temperature before frosting and serving. Take into consideration that the cakes will lose some of their fluffiness if refrigerated or frozen.

Assemble and Decorate

Level the tops of the cakes with a cake cutter or a long, serrated knife as needed.
Line the edges of a cake platter with four strips of parchment paper to keep the platter clean.

Place the first cake layer on the platter. Spread 1 cup of buttercream evenly over the top, and then spread about half of the raspberry jam over the buttercream. Top with the second cake layer, pressing lightly to adhere. Repeat to add the third layer. Then spread the remaining buttercream evenly over the top and sides of the cake. If desired, use a small offset spatula to create a design on the sides of the cake.

Top with fresh raspberries. Remove the parchment paper and serve. The frosted cake can be stored at room temperature for up to 2 days or in the refrigerator for up to 5 days.

EGGLESS TRIPLE-COCONUT CAKE

This Eggless Triple-Coconut Cake has been used to make plenty of birthday wishes at our home. It's two coconut butter-cake layers filled with coconut frosting and shredded coconut, and topped with more frosting and toasted coconut flakes—is your mouth watering yet?

Makes one 2-layer, 8-inch (20-cm) cake, serves 10 to 12

For the Eggless Coconut Cake

4 cups (560 g) all-purpose flour

1 tablespoon + 2 teaspoons (20 g) baking powder

1/2 teaspoon (3 g) baking soda

1/2 teaspoon (2 g) salt

2 cups (480 ml) canned coconut milk

2 tablespoons (30 ml) apple cider vinegar

1 cup (230 g) unsalted butter, softened

2 cups (400 g) granulated sugar

1/4 cup (60 g) plain regular yogurt

2 teaspoons (10 ml) coconut extract

1 teaspoon (5 ml) pure vanilla extract

1 cup (100 g) unsweetened shredded coconut

To Assemble and Decorate

1 batch Coconut Frosting (page 163)

1/4 cup (25 g) unsweetened shredded coconut

2 cups (200 g) toasted coconut flakes

Make the Eggless Coconut Cake

Preheat the oven to 350ºF (180ºC). Line two 8-inch (20-cm) round cake pans with parchment paper. Lightly grease with baking spray with flour.

Sift the flour, baking powder, baking soda, and salt together into a large bowl.

In a mixing bowl or liquid measuring cup, combine the coconut milk and vinegar. Set aside.

Using an electric hand mixer or a stand mixer, beat the butter on medium-high speed until creamy, 3 to 4 minutes. Add the sugar and beat on high speed for 4 minutes, until creamed and pale, scraping down the sides and up the bottom of the bowl with a rubber spatula as needed. Then add the yogurt, coconut extract, and vanilla; continue beating to combine, about 1 minute.

Turn the mixer to low and add the flour mixture in three batches, alternating with the coconut milk mixture, beginning and ending with the flour mixture. Beat until just combined, 30 to 45 seconds. Do not overmix. Fold in the unsweetened shredded coconut.

Evenly divide the batter between the prepared pans.

Bake for 30 to 40 minutes, or until a toothpick inserted in the center comes out clean. Let the cakes cool in their pans on wire racks for 10 minutes, and then remove from the pans. Allow the cakes to cool completely, right-side up, on wire racks before removing the parchment paper.

Unfrosted cake layers can be stored at room temperature for up to 2 days or frozen for up to a month; defrost at room temperature before frosting and serving. Take into consideration that the cakes will lose some of their fluffiness if refrigerated or frozen.

Assemble and Decorate

Level the tops of the cakes with a cake cutter or a long, serrated knife as needed.
Line the edges of a cake platter with four strips of parchment paper to keep the platter clean.

Place the first cake layer on the platter. Spread 1-1/2 to 2 cups of frosting evenly over the top, and then sprinkle on the unsweetened shredded coconut. Top with the second cake layer, pressing lightly to adhere. Then spread the remaining frosting evenly over the top and sides of the cake. Gently press toasted coconut flakes onto the cake sides. Remove the parchment paper and serve. The frosted cake can be stored at room temperature for up to 1 day or in the refrigerator for up to 5 days.

ORIANA'S NOTES:

Make sure to use canned coconut milk. Refrigerated coconut milk is more of a beverage than a baking ingredient. It is often watered down and filled with additives, so I recommend avoiding this type of milk for this recipe.

EGGLESS CHOCOLATE TURTLE CAKE

When I think of a decadent dessert, this is one of the first cakes that comes to mind. This moist chocolate cake is filled with Salted Caramel Buttercream, pecans, and chocolate ganache—pure comfort food in dessert form! It's delicious and makes the perfect celebration cake.

Makes one 3-layer, 6-inch (15-cm) cake, serves 10 to 12

For the Eggless Chocolate Cake

2 cups (400 g) granulated sugar

1-1/2 cups (360 ml) buttermilk

1/2 cup (115 g) unsalted butter, melted

1/2 cup (120 ml) vegetable or canola oil

1/2 cup (120 g) sour cream

2 teaspoons (10 ml) pure vanilla extract

2 tablespoons (30 ml) hot water (optional)

2 teaspoons (2 g) instant espresso powder (optional)

2-1/2 cups (350 g) all-purpose flour

3/4 cup (90 g) unsweetened natural cocoa powder

1 tablespoon + 1 teaspoon (16 g) baking powder

1/2 teaspoon (3 g) baking soda

1/2 teaspoon (2 g) salt

To Assemble and Decorate

1 batch Salted Caramel Buttercream (page 156)

1/2 cup (150 g) Salted Caramel (page 166)

1 cup (125 g) chopped pecans

1 batch Chocolate Ganache (page 165)

Make the Eggless Chocolate Cake

Preheat the oven to 350ºF (180ºC). Line three 6-inch (15-cm) round cake pans with parchment paper. Lightly grease with baking spray with flour.

Combine the sugar, buttermilk, melted butter, oil, sour cream, and vanilla extract in a large bowl and whisk together.

In a small bowl, combine the hot water and instant espresso powder, if using. Add to the butter mixture; mix to combine.

Add the flour, cocoa powder, baking powder, baking soda, and salt; stir until just combined.

Evenly divide the batter among the prepared pans.

Bake for 25 to 35 minutes, or until a toothpick inserted in the center comes out clean. Let the cakes cool in their pans on wire racks for 10 minutes, and then remove from the pans. Allow the cakes to cool completely, right-side up, on wire racks before removing the parchment paper.

Unfrosted cake layers can be stored at room temperature for up to 2 days or frozen for up to a month; defrost at room temperature before frosting and serving. Take into consideration that the cakes will lose some of their fluffiness if refrigerated or frozen.

Assemble and Decorate

Level the tops of the cakes with a cake cutter or a long, serrated knife as needed.
Line the edges of a cake platter with four strips of parchment paper to keep the platter clean.

Place the first cake layer on the platter. Spread 1 cup of buttercream evenly over the top. Drizzle with 1/4 cup salted caramel and top with 1/2 cup chopped pecans. Top with the second cake layer, pressing lightly to adhere. Add the third layer, and then spread 1 cup of frosting evenly over the top of the third layer, leaving the sides unfrosted.

Add the ganache drip. Use a spoon to add the ganache around the top edge of the cake and gently push it over the edge so it falls, creating a drip. Continue adding drips around the outer edge until you've gone all the way around. Then fill in the center, pouring the remaining ganache onto the top of the cake and using your offset spatula to spread it evenly. Refrigerate the cake for 15 minutes to set the drip.

Place the remaining buttercream in a piping bag fitted with your favorite piping tip. Add as many swirls on the top of the cake as you like. Top with more chopped pecans if desired. Remove the parchment paper strips and serve. The frosted cake can be stored at room temperature for up to 2 days or in the refrigerator for up to 5 days.

ORIANA'S NOTES:

Salted caramel keeps very well in the fridge, so you can make this part ahead of time or make a big batch and save it for later use.

EGGLESS GINGERBREAD BUNDT CAKE

We love Christmas at our home and have tried our best to keep a few of our favorite holiday traditions going with our kids. Eggless Gingerbread Bundt Cake, with its traditional gingerbread-cookie flavor in Bundt-cake form, is a tradition we never skip. Serve this gorgeous cake at brunch or for dessert—either way, it's a guaranteed showstopper.

Makes one 12-cup Bundt cake, serves 10 to 12

4 cups (560 g) all-purpose flour

1 tablespoon + 1 teaspoon (16 g) baking powder

1/2 teaspoon (3 g) baking soda

1/2 teaspoon (2 g) salt

2 teaspoons (4 g) ground cinnamon

1 teaspoon (2 g) ground ginger

1 teaspoon (2 g) ground nutmeg

1-1/2 cups (360 ml) milk

2 tablespoons (30 ml) apple cider vinegar

1 cup (230 g) unsalted butter, softened

1 cup (200 g) brown sugar

1 cup (320 g) unsulphured molasses

2 teaspoons (10 ml) pure vanilla extract

1/4 cup (30 g) confectioners' sugar (optional)

Preheat the oven to 350ºF (180ºC). Spray a 12-cup, nonstick Bundt pan with baking spray with flour.

Sift the flour, baking powder, baking soda, salt, cinnamon, ginger, and nutmeg together into a large bowl.

In a mixing bowl or liquid measuring cup, combine the milk and vinegar. Let the mixture rest for 5 to 8 minutes, until thickened and curdled.

Using an electric hand mixer or a stand mixer, beat the butter on medium-high speed until creamy, 3 to 4 minutes. Add the brown sugar and beat on high speed for 4 minutes, until creamed and smooth, scraping down the sides and up the bottom of the bowl with a rubber spatula as needed. Then add the molasses and vanilla; continue beating until well combined, about 2 minutes.

Turn the mixer to low and add the flour mixture in three batches, alternating with the milk mixture, beginning and ending with the flour mixture. Beat until just combined, 30 to 45 seconds. Do not overmix. Give the batter a final stir by hand to ensure everything is well combined.

Spoon the batter into the prepared pan and smooth the top.

Bake for 50 to 60 minutes, or until a toothpick inserted in the center comes out clean. Let the cake cool in the pan on a wire rack for 20 minutes, and then remove from the pan. Allow the cake to cool completely on a wire rack before slicing. Sprinkle with confectioners' sugar, if desired, and serve.

The cake can be stored at room temperature for up to 3 days or frozen for up to a month; defrost at room temperature before serving. Take into consideration that the cake will lose some of its fluffiness if refrigerated or frozen.

Scan with your phone for my **Eggless Gingerbread Cookies Recipe**

ORIANA'S NOTES:

You can use light or dark molasses in this recipe, but avoid using bitter blackstrap molasses.
You can also bake this cake in a decorative 10-cup Bundt pan; place a baking sheet under the Bundt pan to catch any drips.

EGGLESS COOKIES-AND-CREAM CHEESECAKE

Everyone loves classic cheesecake, but this Eggless Cookies-and-Cream Cheesecake takes it to a whole new level of yumminess. At least that's what my youngest daughter says; it's her favorite recipe in the whole book. She is quite the cheesecake fanatic, and for this easy-to-make dessert, I combined two of her favorites: cheesecake and Oreos.

Makes one 9-inch (23-cm) cheesecake, serves 10 to 12

For the Crust

1-3/4 cups (175 g) graham cracker crumbs (from about 27 graham cracker squares)

5 tablespoons (75 g) unsalted butter, melted

2 tablespoons (25 g) granulated sugar

For the Eggless Cookies-and-Cream Filling

3 tablespoons (30 g) cornstarch

3 tablespoons (45 ml) water

24 ounces (678 g) full-fat cream cheese, softened

1/2 cup (100 g) granulated sugar

1/2 cup (120 g) sour cream

1 14-ounce (398 g) can sweetened condensed milk

1/2 cup (120 ml) heavy whipping cream

2 teaspoons (10 ml) pure vanilla extract

20 Oreo cookies, coarsely chopped

To Decorate

1 cup (240 ml) whipped cream

Chopped Oreos to taste

ORIANA'S NOTES:

After many years of cheesecake making, I have concluded that most springform pans leak, so to avoid water leaks, I like to wrap the springform pan with a slow cooker liner. I place the springform pan in the middle of the slow cooker liner, grab all the excess, wind it up, and tie the end with a knot. Finally, I add aluminum foil for double coverage.

Make the Crust

Lightly grease a 9-inch (23-cm) round springform pan and line it with parchment paper.

In a medium mixing bowl, combine the graham cracker crumbs, butter, and sugar with a fork until evenly moistened.

Pour the crumb mixture into the prepared pan and press down into the base and up the sides. Refrigerate for at least 15 minutes while you make the filling.

Make the Eggless Cookies-and-Cream Filling

Preheat the oven to 350ºF (180ºC).

Combine the cornstarch and water in a small bowl and mix until smooth. Set aside.

Using an electric hand mixer or a stand mixer, beat the cream cheese on low speed for 2 to 3 minutes, until smooth and free of any lumps. Add the sugar and sour cream and continue mixing until incorporated. Gradually add the sweetened condensed milk and beat until creamy, 1 to 2 minutes. Add the heavy cream, vanilla, and cornstarch mixture; beat on medium-high speed for 2 minutes. Fold in the chopped Oreo cookies.

Pour the mixture onto the crust and tap gently on the counter to remove any air bubbles.

Place the cheesecake pan on a large piece of aluminum foil and fold the foil up around the sides of the pan (this is to keep the water from seeping into the cheesecake). Place the cake pan in a large roasting pan. Pour hot water into the roasting pan until the water is about halfway up the cheesecake pan's sides.

Bake for 40 minutes, or until the edges are just barely puffed. When the initial 40 minutes of baking is over, turn off the oven and leave the cheesecake inside the hot oven with the door closed for 40 more minutes. The cheesecake will continue to cook, but will slowly begin to cool as well. After 40 minutes, remove the cheesecake from the oven. The center should still wobble when you remove it.

Remove the cheesecake from the water bath and the wrapping. Let it cool in the pan until it reaches room temperature, and then refrigerate in the pan for at least 4 hours or overnight. When ready to serve, loosen the cheesecake from the pan's sides by running a thin metal spatula around the inside rim. Unmold and transfer to a cake plate.

Decorate

Just before serving, top the cheesecake with whipped cream; sprinkle with crushed cookies. Store in the refrigerator for up to 5 days.

Scan with your phone for my **Eggless Classic Cheesecake Recipe**

ULTIMATE EGGLESS RAINBOW CAKE

This colorful layer cake is ideal for a child's birthday celebration. Six layers of rainbow-colored eggless vanilla cake are piled high—filled, frosted, and decorated with delicious American Vanilla Buttercream; and covered with a pink white-chocolate drip and sprinkles. The result is impressive, bright, and happy. Don't feel intimidated—it's easier to make than it looks!

Makes one 6-layer, 6-inch (15-cm) cake, serves 16 to 20

For the Eggless Rainbow Cake

6 cups (840 g) all-purpose flour

2 tablespoons + 1 teaspoon (28 g) baking powder

1 teaspoon (6 g) baking soda

1 teaspoon (4 g) salt

3 cups (720 ml) milk

3 tablespoons (45 ml) apple cider vinegar

1-1/2 cups (345 g) unsalted butter, softened

3 cups (600 g) granulated sugar

1/3 cup + 2 tablespoons (90 g) plain regular yogurt

1 tablespoon (15 ml) pure vanilla extract

6 different colors gel food coloring

For the Pink Ganache Drip

1/3 cup (80 ml) heavy cream

1 cup (200 g) white chocolate chips

Pink gel food coloring

To Assemble and Decorate

2 batches American Vanilla Buttercream (page 145)

1/2 cup (95 g) sprinkles

Make the Eggless Rainbow Cake

Preheat the oven to 350ºF (180ºC). Line six 6-inch (15-cm) round cake pans with parchment paper. Lightly grease with baking spray with flour.

Sift the flour, baking powder, baking soda, and salt together into a large bowl.

In a mixing bowl or liquid measuring cup, combine the milk and vinegar. Let the mixture rest for 5 to 8 minutes, until thickened and curdled.

Using an electric hand mixer or a stand mixer, beat the butter on medium-high speed until creamy, 3 to 4 minutes. Add the sugar and beat on high speed for 4 minutes, until creamed and pale, scraping down the sides and up the bottom of the bowl with a rubber spatula as needed. Then add the yogurt and vanilla; continue beating to combine, about 1 minute.

Turn the mixer to low and add the flour mixture in three batches, alternating with the milk mixture, beginning and ending with the flour mixture. Beat until just combined, 30 to 45 seconds. Do not overmix.

Evenly divide the batter into 6 different batches. Color each with drops of food coloring until you reach the desired colors.

Bake layers for 23 to 28 minutes, or until a toothpick inserted in the center comes out clean. Let the cakes cool in their pans on wire racks for 10 minutes, and then remove from the pans. Allow the cakes to cool completely, right-side up, on wire racks before removing the parchment paper.

Unfrosted cake layers can be stored at room temperature for up to 2 days or frozen for up to a month; defrost at room temperature before frosting and serving. Take into consideration that the cakes will lose some of their fluffiness if refrigerated or frozen.

Make the Pink Ganache Drip

Heat the heavy cream in the microwave for 45 seconds. Add the white chocolate chips and let rest for 1 to 2 minutes. Then stir until smooth. Add enough gel food coloring to achieve the desired color and mix well to incorporate.

ORIANA'S NOTES:

You can also use candy melts to make the pink drip; follow the packet instructions.

If you don't have six cake pans, I would recommend making a half batch and baking the first three layers. Then, while the first three layers are cooling, make the second batch.

Assemble and Decorate

Level the tops of the cakes with a cake cutter or a long, serrated knife as needed.

Line the edges of a cake platter with four strips of parchment paper to keep the platter clean.

Place the first cake layer on the platter. Spread 1 cup of buttercream over the top. Top with the second cake layer, pressing to adhere, and then repeat to stack all six layers. Frost the top and sides of the cake with 2–3 cups buttercream. You can smooth the cake's top and sides with the edge of an offset spatula to smooth out any bumps.

Refrigerate the cake for 15 to 20 minutes.

Add the ganache drip. Use a spoon to add the ganache around the top edge of the cake and gently push it over the edge so it falls, creating a drip. Continue adding drips around the outer edge until you've gone all the way around. Then fill in the center, pouring the remaining ganache onto the top of the cake and using your offset spatula to spread it evenly.

Place the remaining buttercream in a piping bag fitted with your favorite piping tip. Add as many swirls or rosettes on top of the cake as you like, and then top with sprinkles. Remove the parchment paper and serve. The frosted cake can be stored at room temperature for up to 2 days or in the refrigerator for up to 5 days.

EGGLESS CHOCOLATE PEPPERMINT CAKE

Chocolate and peppermint are a classic Christmas combination. And since so many of my readers have requested peppermint recipes, I knew I needed to create a gorgeous layer cake—something worthy of the occasion. After all, Christmas is a big deal in our home! My kids love this cake, and even my husband, who doesn't usually care for peppermint, licked the plate clean after eating this one.

Makes one 3-layer, 6-inch (15-cm) cake, serves 10 to 12

For the Eggless Chocolate Peppermint Cake

2 cups (400 g) granulated sugar

1-1/2 cups (360 ml) buttermilk

1/2 cup (115 g) unsalted butter, melted

1/2 cup (120 ml) vegetable or canola oil

1/2 cup (120 g) sour cream

2 teaspoons (10 ml) pure vanilla extract

1 teaspoon (5 ml) peppermint extract

2 tablespoons (30 ml) hot water (optional)

2 teaspoons (2 g) instant espresso powder (optional)

2-1/2 cups (350 g) all-purpose flour

3/4 cup (90 g) unsweetened natural cocoa powder

1 tablespoon + 1 teaspoon (16 g) baking powder

1/2 teaspoon (3 g) baking soda

1/2 teaspoon (2 g) salt

To Assemble and Decorate

1 medium batch Eggless White Chocolate Swiss Meringue Buttercream (page 154)

10 to 12 peppermint candies, coarsely chopped

5 to 6 peppermint bark squares

Make the Eggless Chocolate Peppermint Cake

Preheat the oven to 350ºF (180ºC). Line three 6-inch (15-cm) round cake pans with parchment paper. Lightly grease with baking spray with flour.

Combine the sugar, buttermilk, melted butter, oil, sour cream, vanilla, and peppermint extract in a large bowl and whisk together.

In a small bowl, combine the hot water and instant espresso powder, if using. Add to the butter mixture; mix to combine.

Add the flour, cocoa powder, baking powder, baking soda, and salt; stir until just combined.

Evenly divide the batter among the prepared pans.

Bake for 30 to 40 minutes, or until a toothpick inserted in the center comes out clean. Let the cakes cool in their pans on wire racks for 10 minutes, and then remove from the pans. Allow the cakes to cool completely, right-side up, on wire racks before removing the parchment paper.

Unfrosted cake layers can be stored at room temperature for up to 24 hours or frozen for up to a month; defrost at room temperature before frosting and serving. Take into consideration that the cakes will lose some of their fluffiness if refrigerated or frozen.

Assemble and Decorate

Level the tops of the cakes with a cake cutter or a long, serrated knife as needed.

Line the edges of a cake platter with four strips of parchment paper to keep the platter clean.

Place the first cake layer on the platter. Spread 1 cup of buttercream evenly over the top. Top with the second cake layer, pressing lightly to adhere. Repeat to add the third layer. Then spread about 1-1/2 cups buttercream evenly over the top and sides of the cake. You can smooth the cake's top and sides with the edge of an offset spatula to smooth out any bumps.

Gently press the chopped peppermint candies onto the lower part of the sides of the cake. Arrange the peppermint bark squares on top. Remove the parchment paper strips and serve. The frosted cake can be stored at room temperature for up to 2 days or in the refrigerator for up to 5 days.

ORIANA'S NOTES:

If you want to boost the peppermint flavor in this cake, I recommend adding 1/2 teaspoon peppermint extract to the buttercream.

EGGLESS SPICED RUM SHEET CAKE

This Eggless Spiced Rum Sheet Cake has a moist crumb that balances well with the creamy cinnamon frosting and crunchy cookie pieces in every bite. It's drenched in rum flavor without being overpowering. I've included a rum syrup that can be brushed over the cake as soon as it comes out of the oven, but it's totally optional. If you choose to omit the syrup, the cake will still be delicious; it will just have a subtler rum flavor.

Makes one 9 x 13 inch (24 x 35 cm) cake, serves 12 to 16

For the Eggless Spiced Rum Sheet Cake

4 cups (560 g) all-purpose flour

1 tablespoon + 1 teaspoon (16 g) baking powder

1/2 teaspoon (3 g) baking soda

1/2 teaspoon (2 g) salt

2 teaspoons (4 g) ground cinnamon

1 teaspoon (2 g) ground ginger

1 teaspoon (2 g) ground nutmeg

1/2 teaspoon (1 g) ground allspice

1/8 teaspoon (0.5 g) ground cloves

1/8 teaspoon (0.5 g) ground cardamom

1-1/2 cups (360 ml) milk

2 tablespoons (30 ml) apple cider vinegar

1 cup (230 g) unsalted butter, softened

1 cup (200 g) brown sugar

1 cup (320 g) unsulphured molasses

2 tablespoons (30 ml) spiced rum

2 teaspoons (10 ml) pure vanilla extract

1 teaspoon (5 ml) rum extract

For the Rum Syrup (optional)

2/3 cup (94 g) unsalted butter

1/2 cup (100 g) granulated sugar

2 tablespoons (30 ml) water

1/4 teaspoon (1 g) salt

1/4 cup (60 ml) dark or spiced rum

To Decorate

1 batch Cinnamon Buttercream (page 157)

Biscoff cookies, crumbled

Make the Eggless Spiced Rum Sheet Cake

Preheat the oven to 350°F (180°C). Line a 9 x 13 inch (24 x 35 cm) baking pan with parchment paper. Lightly grease with baking spray with flour.

Sift the flour, baking powder, baking soda, salt, cinnamon, ginger, nutmeg, allspice, cloves, and cardamom together into a large bowl.

In a mixing bowl or liquid measuring cup, combine the milk and vinegar. Let the mixture rest for 5 to 8 minutes, until thickened and curdled.

Using an electric hand mixer or a stand mixer, beat the butter on medium-high speed until creamy, 3 to 4 minutes. Add the brown sugar and beat on high speed for 4 minutes, until creamed and smooth, scraping down the sides and up the bottom of the bowl with a rubber spatula as needed. Then add the molasses, rum, vanilla, and rum extract; continue beating until well combined, about 2 minutes.

Turn the mixer to low and add the flour mixture in three batches, alternating with the milk mixture, beginning and ending with the flour mixture. Beat until just combined, 30 to 45 seconds. Do not overmix. Give the batter a final stir by hand to ensure everything is well combined.

Transfer the batter to the prepared pan and smooth the top with a rubber spatula.

Bake for 50 to 60 minutes, or until a toothpick inserted in the center comes out clean.

Meanwhile, make the Rum Syrup, if using.

Melt the butter in a small saucepan over medium heat. Once it is melted, stir in the sugar, water, and salt. Boil for 5 minutes, stirring constantly. Turn off the heat and stir in the rum. Then return the pan to medium heat for 30 to 45 seconds. Remove from the heat and set aside to cool slightly.

As soon as the cake comes out of the oven, brush the syrup over the cake. Let the cake cool completely in the pan on a wire rack.

Decorate

Frost the cooled cake with the cinnamon buttercream, smoothing the top with an offset spatula and sprinkling the top with crumbled Biscoff cookies. Slice and serve. The frosted cake can be stored at room temperature for up to 2 days or in the refrigerator for 5 days.

> **ORIANA'S NOTES:**
>
> You can also decorate this cake with chopped nuts or cinnamon chips, if you prefer.

EGGLESS NEAPOLITAN CAKE

Neapolitan is a combination of vanilla, chocolate, and strawberry. I love this Eggless Neapolitan Cake, especially because it is made using just one cake batter! The cake batter is divided into three—one batch stays as it is, another is flavored with strawberry puree, and the final batch gets a touch of cocoa powder. Gorgeous to look at and even better to eat, this fantastic cake is equally at home at a family gathering, an elegant dinner party, or a holiday celebration.

Makes one 3-layer, 6-inch (15-cm) cake, serves 10 to 12

For the Eggless Neapolitan Cake

8 ounces (225 g) fresh strawberries, washed and hulled

4 cups (560 g) all-purpose flour

1 tablespoon + 2 teaspoons (20 g) baking powder

1/2 teaspoon (3 g) baking soda

1/2 teaspoon (2 g) salt

2 cups (480 ml) milk

2 tablespoons (30 ml) apple cider vinegar

1 cup (230 g) unsalted butter, softened

2 cups (400 g) granulated sugar

1/4 cup (60 g) plain regular yogurt

2 teaspoons (10 ml) pure vanilla extract

1/3 cup (80 ml) hot water

1/4 cup (30 g) unsweetened cocoa powder

1/2 teaspoon (0.5 g) instant espresso powder

To Assemble and Decorate

1 medium batch Eggless Vanilla Swiss Meringue Buttercream (page 152)

1 batch Chocolate Ganache (page 165)

1/4 cup (48 g) sprinkles

Make the Eggless Neapolitan Cake

Puree the strawberries in a food processor or blender until smooth.

Transfer the strawberry puree to a saucepan or skillet. Cook over medium heat, stirring constantly, until mixture begins to thicken and bubble, 5 to 10 minutes. Reduce the heat to medium-low and allow the strawberry mixture to simmer for 10 to15 minutes, until reduced by half. Remove from the heat, pour into a bowl, and set aside to cool.

Preheat the oven to 350ºF (180ºC). Line three 6-inch (15-cm) round cake pans with parchment paper. Lightly grease with baking spray with flour.

Sift the flour, baking powder, baking soda, and salt together into a large bowl.

In a mixing bowl or liquid measuring cup, combine the milk and vinegar. Let the mixture rest for 5 to 8 minutes, until thickened and curdled.

Using an electric hand mixer or a stand mixer, beat the butter on medium-high speed until creamy, 3 to 4 minutes. Add the sugar and beat on high speed for 4 minutes until creamed and pale, scraping down the sides and up the bottom of the bowl with a rubber spatula as needed. Then add the yogurt and vanilla; continue beating to combine, about 1 minute.

Turn the mixer to low and add the flour mixture in three batches, alternating with the milk mixture, beginning and ending with the flour mixture. Beat until just combined, 30 to 45 seconds. Do not overmix.

Evenly divide the batter into three batches.

Add the hot water, cocoa powder, and espresso powder to one batch; mix to combine.

Add 1/4 cup (65 g) strawberry puree to the second batch; mix to combine.

Transfer the three batters into the prepared pans.

Bake for 30 to 35 minutes, or until a toothpick inserted in the center comes out clean. Let the cakes cool in their pans on wire racks for 10 minutes, and then remove from the pans. Allow the cakes to cool completely, right-side up, on wire racks before removing the parchment paper.

Unfrosted cake layers can be stored at room temperature for up to 2 days or frozen for up to a month; defrost at room temperature before frosting and serving. Take into consideration that the cakes will lose some of their fluffiness if refrigerated or frozen.

> **ORIANA'S NOTES:**
>
> The cake layers might be done at different times, so keep a close eye on them and make sure the centers are set before removing the pans from the oven.

Assemble and Decorate

Level the tops of the cakes with a cake cutter or a long, serrated knife as needed.

Line the edges of a cake platter with four strips of parchment paper to keep the platter clean.

Place the chocolate layer on the platter. Spread 1 cup of buttercream evenly over the top. Top with the strawberry layer, pressing lightly to adhere. Repeat to add the vanilla layer. Then spread about 1-1/2 cups buttercream evenly over the top and sides of the cake. You can smooth the cake's top and sides with the edge of an offset spatula to smooth out any bumps. Refrigerate the cake for 15 minutes.

Add the ganache drip. Use a spoon to add the ganache around the top edge of the cake and gently push it over the edge so it falls, creating a drip. Continue adding drips around the outer edge until you've gone all the way around. Then fill in the center, pouring the remaining ganache onto the top of the cake and using your offset spatula to spread it evenly. Refrigerate the cake for 15 minutes to set the drip.

Place the remaining buttercream in a piping bag fitted with your favorite piping tip. Add as many swirls or rosettes on the top of the cake as you like, and then top with sprinkles. Remove the parchment paper and serve.

EGGLESS GERMAN CHOCOLATE SHEET CAKE

This Eggless German Chocolate Cake is simply dreamy—super moist, rich, and totally decadent, frosted with a nutty and buttery coconut-pecan topping that is to die for. Every time I make a sheet cake, I wonder why I don't make them more often. They're the perfect answer to potlucks and parties since they serve a good number of people. They're also easy to make, and everyone loves them!

Makes one 9 x 13 inch (24 x 35 cm) cake, serves 12 to 16

For the Eggless Chocolate Sheet Cake

2 cups (400 g) granulated sugar

1-1/2 cups (360 ml) buttermilk

1/2 cup (115 g) unsalted butter, melted

1/2 cup (120 ml) vegetable or canola oil

1/2 cup (120 g) sour cream

2 teaspoons (10 ml) pure vanilla extract

2 tablespoons (30 ml) hot water (optional)

2 teaspoons (2 g) instant espresso powder (optional)

2-1/2 cups (350 g) all-purpose flour

3/4 cup (90 g) unsweetened natural cocoa powder

1 tablespoon + 1 teaspoon (16 g) baking powder

1/2 teaspoon (3 g) baking soda

1/2 teaspoon (2 g) salt

For the Coconut-Pecan Topping

6 ounces (178 ml) evaporated milk

1 tablespoon (10 g) cornstarch

1/3 cup (80 g) unsalted butter

3/4 cup (150 g) brown sugar

1 teaspoon (5 ml) pure vanilla extract

1 cup (100 g) unsweetened shredded or flaked coconut

3/4 cup (93 g) toasted pecans, coarsely chopped

To Assemble and Decorate

1/2 batch American Chocolate Buttercream (page 145)

Scan with your phone for my **2-layer Eggless German Chocolate Cake** recipe

Make the Eggless Chocolate Sheet Cake

Preheat the oven to 350ºF (180ºC). Line a 9 x 13 inch (24 x 35 cm) baking pan with parchment paper. Lightly grease with baking spray with flour.

Combine the sugar, buttermilk, melted butter, oil, sour cream, and vanilla extract in a large bowl and whisk together.

In a small bowl, combine the hot water and instant espresso powder, if using. Add to the butter mixture; mix to combine.

Add the flour, cocoa powder, baking powder, baking soda, and salt; stir until just combined.

Transfer the batter into the prepared pan.

Bake for 40 to 45 minutes, or until a toothpick inserted in the center comes out clean. Let the cake cool completely in the pan on a wire rack.

Unfrosted cake can be stored at room temperature for up to 2 days or frozen for up to a month; defrost at room temperature before frosting and serving. Take into consideration that the cake will lose some of its fluffiness if refrigerated or frozen.

Make the Coconut-Pecan Topping

In a small bowl, combine 2 tablespoons of the evaporated milk and the cornstarch. Stir to mix and set aside.

In a medium saucepan over medium heat, combine the remaining evaporated milk, the butter, and the brown sugar. Whisk occasionally as the mixture comes to a low boil. Once boiling, stir in the cornstarch mixture and whisk constantly until the mixture thickens a little, 2 to 3 minutes.

Remove from the heat and stir in the vanilla, coconut, and pecans. Allow to cool completely before topping the cake.

Assemble and Decorate

Frost the cooled cake with an even layer of chocolate buttercream. Evenly spread the coconut-pecan topping on top. Slice and serve. The frosted cake can be stored at room temperature for up to 1 day or in the refrigerator for 5 days.

> **ORIANA'S NOTES:**
>
> You can also use Baker's German's Sweet Chocolate to make this cake. To do so, reduce the cocoa powder to 2 tablespoons (15 g) and the oil to 1/4 cup + 3 tablespoons (105 ml). Melt 4 ounces of Baker's German's Sweet Chocolate and add it to the wet ingredients in step 2.

EGGLESS CREAM CHEESE COFFEE CAKE

There is nothing more appealing to me than a cup of coffee and a piece of coffee cake. This delicious, melt-in-your-mouth eggless coffee cake has a ribbon of cream cheese filling and a crisp streusel topping. It's a perfect breakfast, brunch, or midafternoon treat.

Makes one 9-inch (23-cm) cake, serves 10 to 12

For the Streusel Topping

1/2 cup (70 g) all-purpose flour

1/3 cup (67 g) brown sugar

1 teaspoon (3 g) ground cinnamon

1/4 teaspoon (1 g) salt

3 tablespoons (42 g) unsalted butter, cold and cubed

For the Cream Cheese Filling

16 ounces (454 g) cream cheese, softened

1/2 cup (100 g) granulated sugar

1/4 cup (35 g) all-purpose flour

For the Eggless Cream Cheese Coffee Cake

2-1/2 cups (350 g) all-purpose flour

2 teaspoons (8 g) baking powder

1/2 teaspoon (3 g) baking soda

1/2 teaspoon (2 g) salt

8 ounces (225 g) cream cheese, softened

1/2 cup (115 g) unsalted butter, softened

1 cup (200 g) brown sugar

1/2 cup (100 g) granulated sugar

1/3 cup (80 g) plain yogurt

2 teaspoons (10 ml) pure vanilla extract

1/2 cup (120 ml) buttermilk

To Decorate

1 batch Sugar Glaze (page 169)

Make the Streusel Topping

Combine the flour, brown sugar, cinnamon, and salt in a bowl. Cut in the butter using a pastry cutter or rub in with your fingers until small to medium clumps form. Set aside.

Make the Cream Cheese Filling

Using an electric hand mixer or a stand mixer, beat the cream cheese, sugar, and flour over medium speed until creamy and smooth. Set aside.

Make the Eggless Cream Cheese Coffee Cake

Preheat the oven to 350ºF (180ºC). Lightly grease a 9-inch (23-cm) springform pan and line it with parchment paper. I use a square springform pan.

In a large bowl, combine the flour, baking powder, baking soda, and salt. Set aside.

Using an electric hand mixer or a stand mixer, beat the cream cheese, butter, and sugars on medium-high speed until creamy, 5 to 6 minutes, scraping down the sides and up the bottom of the bowl with a rubber spatula as needed. Then add the yogurt and vanilla; continue beating to combine, about 1 minute.

Turn the mixer to low and add the flour mixture in three batches, alternating with the buttermilk, beginning and ending with the flour mixture. Beat until just combined, 30 to 45 seconds. Do not overmix.

Spread half of the batter into the prepared pan with a spatula. Dollop the cream cheese filling over the batter and evenly spread it. Dollop the remaining batter over the cream cheese layer and use a spatula to spread it evenly and smooth the top.

Roll the streusel topping between your thumb and forefinger into large pea-size pieces. Spread the pieces in an even layer over the batter.

Bake for 40 to 50 minutes, or until a toothpick inserted in the center comes out clean and the streusel is golden. Allow to cool for 10 minutes, and then remove the sides of the springform pan and allow the cake to cool completely before glazing.

Decorate

Drizzle the sugar glaze over the top. Serve. The cake can be stored at room temperature for up to 3 days or in the refrigerator for 5 days.

> **ORIANA'S NOTES:**
>
> To add another layer of flavor to your cake, you can add 1/2 cup chopped nuts, such as pecans, walnuts, or almonds, to the streusel.

EGGLESS BROWN SUGAR MARBLE BUNDT CAKE

Brown sugar can change the simplest recipe into something decadent. This Eggless Brown Sugar Marble Bundt Cake is tender and just sweet enough, with a bit of chocolate flavor. Normally I make my cakes in plain round cake pans, but since this cake is more like a pound cake in density, it does really well in a Bundt pan. Plus, Bundt pans are normally decorative, so there's no need to frost it. This cake is perfect with a glass of milk or a cup of coffee or tea.

Makes one 12-cup Bundt cake, serves 10 to 12

3 cups (420 g) all-purpose flour

1 tablespoon + 1 teaspoon (16 g) baking powder

1/2 teaspoon (3 g) baking soda

1/2 teaspoon (2 g) salt

1-1/2 cups (360 ml) milk

1-1/2 tablespoons (22.5 ml) apple cider vinegar

3/4 cup (174 g) unsalted butter, softened

3/4 cup (150 g) granulated sugar

3/4 cup (150 g) brown sugar

2 teaspoons (10 ml) pure vanilla extract

1/3 cup (80 ml) hot water

1/4 cup (25 g) natural unsweetened cocoa powder

1 teaspoon (1g) instant espresso powder (optional)

Preheat the oven to 350°F (180°C). Spray a 12-cup nonstick Bundt pan with baking spray with flour.

Sift the flour, baking powder, baking soda, and salt together into a large bowl.

In a mixing bowl or liquid measuring cup, combine the milk and vinegar. Let the mixture rest for 5 to 8 minutes, until thickened and curdled.

Using an electric hand mixer or a stand mixer, beat the butter on medium-high speed until creamy, 3 to 4 minutes. Add the granulated sugar and beat on high speed for 4 minutes, until creamed and smooth, scraping down the sides and up the bottom of the bowl with a rubber spatula as needed. Then add the brown sugar and vanilla; continue beating until well combined, about 2 minutes.

Turn the mixer to low and add the flour mixture in three batches, alternating with the milk mixture, beginning and ending with the flour mixture. Beat until just combined, 30 to 45 seconds. Do not overmix. Give batter a final stir by hand to ensure everything is well combined.

Transfer 2 cups of the batter to a bowl.

In a small bowl, stir together the hot water, cocoa powder, and espresso powder, if using. Add this mixture to the reserved 2 cups batter; mix well to combine.

Add a spoonful of each of the batters alternately to the prepared Bundt pan. Using a butter knife, swirl the batters together with a zigzag motion two times. It's important not to over-swirl, or you won't be able to get the marble effect in your cake.

Bake for 50 to 60 minutes, or until a toothpick inserted in the center comes out clean. Let the cake cool in the pan on a wire rack for 20 minutes, and then remove from the pan. Allow the cake to cool completely on a wire rack before slicing.

The cake can be stored at room temperature for up to 3 days or frozen for up to a month; defrost at room temperature before serving. Take into consideration that the cake will lose some of its fluffiness if refrigerated or frozen.

ORIANA'S NOTES:

You can also bake this cake in a decorative 10-cup Bundt pan; place a baking sheet under the Bundt pan to catch any drips.

EGGLESS OREO CAKE

This Oreo cake is beyond delicious! Oreos have been one of my daughter's favorite cookies for probably forever. So for her last birthday, I whipped up my eggless vanilla cake, folded in chopped Oreos, and a delicious cake was born. It is full of crushed Oreos and frosted with Oreo buttercream—an Oreo lover's dream!

Makes one 3-layer, 7-inch (18-cm) cake, serves 10 to 12

For the Eggless Oreo Cake

4 cups (560 g) all-purpose flour

1 tablespoon + 2 teaspoons (20 g) baking powder

1/2 teaspoon (3 g) baking soda

1/2 teaspoon (2 g) salt

2 cups (480 ml) milk

2 tablespoons (30 ml) apple cider vinegar

1 cup (230 g) unsalted butter, softened

2 cups (400 g) granulated sugar

1/4 cup (60 g) plain regular yogurt

2 teaspoons (10 ml) pure vanilla extract

12 to 14 Oreo cookies, crushed (about 120 g)

To Assemble and Decorate

2 batches Oreo Buttercream (page 158)

1 batch Chocolate Ganache (page 165)

6 to 8 Mini Oreo cookies

Make the Eggless Oreo Cake

Preheat the oven to 350°F (180°C). Line three 7-inch (18-cm) round cake pans with parchment paper. Lightly grease with baking spray with flour.

Sift the flour, baking powder, baking soda, and salt together into a large bowl.

In a mixing bowl or liquid measuring cup, combine the milk and vinegar. Let the mixture rest for 5 to 8 minutes, until thickened and curdled.

Using an electric hand mixer or a stand mixer, beat the butter on medium-high speed until creamy, 3 to 4 minutes. Add the sugar and beat on high speed for 4 minutes, until creamed and pale, scraping down the sides and up the bottom of the bowl with a rubber spatula as needed. Then add the yogurt and vanilla; continue beating to combine, about 1 minute.

Turn the mixer to low and add the flour mixture in three batches, alternating with the milk mixture, beginning and ending with the flour mixture. Beat until just combined, 30 to 45 seconds. Do not overmix. Fold in the crushed Oreos.

Evenly divide the batter among the prepared pans.

Bake for 35 to 45 minutes, or until a toothpick inserted in the center comes out clean. Let the cakes cool in their pans on wire racks for 10 minutes, and then remove from the pans. Allow the cakes to cool completely, right-side up, on wire racks before removing the parchment paper.

Unfrosted cake layers can be stored at room temperature for up to 2 days or frozen for up to a month; defrost at room temperature before frosting and serving. Take into consideration that the cakes will lose some of their fluffiness if refrigerated or frozen.

Assemble and Decorate

Level the tops of the cakes with a cake cutter or a long, serrated knife as needed.

Line the edges of a cake platter with four strips of parchment paper to keep the platter clean.

Place the first cake layer on the platter. Spread 1 cup buttercream evenly over the top. Place the second cake layer on top, pressing lightly to adhere. Repeat to add the third layer. Then spread about 1-1/2 cups buttercream evenly over the top and sides of the cake. You can smooth the cake's top and sides with the edge of an offset spatula to smooth out any bumps. Refrigerate the cake for 15 minutes.

Add the chocolate ganache drip. Use a spoon to add the ganache around the top edge of the cake and gently push it over the edge so it falls, creating a drip. Continue adding drips around the outer edge until you've gone all the way around. Then fill in the center, pouring the remaining ganache onto the top of the cake and using your offset spatula to spread it evenly. Refrigerate the cake for 15 minutes to set the drip.

Place the remaining buttercream in a piping bag fitted with your favorite piping tip. Add as many swirls or rosettes on the top of the cake as you like, and then top with Mini Oreos. Remove the parchment paper and serve. The frosted cake can be stored at room temperature for up to 2 days or in the refrigerator for 5 days.

ORIANA'S NOTES:

To take this cake to the next level, add crushed Oreos between layers.

EGGLESS BURNT BASQUE CHEESECAKE

This Eggless Burnt Basque Cheesecake has undoubtedly been my most-requested recipe recently. When I first heard of Basque cheesecake, I didn't know what it was, but I thought, if it's a cheesecake, it must be good! So I began to research and test, and I couldn't be happier about the results. My whole family loves this recipe. Basque cheesecake originated in Spain and is a crustless cheesecake that is cooked at very high heat. This gives it its rustic appearance, with cracked edges and an almost burnt surface. It is wonderfully creamy, light, and smooth. You need to try it soon!

Makes one 9-inch (23-cm) cheesecake, serves 10 to 12

20 ounces (580 g) full-fat cream cheese

1/2 cup (120 g) Greek yogurt

1/2 cup (100 g) granulated sugar

1 14-ounce (397 g) can sweetened condensed milk

1 cup (240 ml) heavy whipping cream

2 teaspoons (10 ml) pure vanilla extract

1/4 cup + 1 tablespoon (50 g) milk powder

1/2 teaspoon (2 g) baking powder

1/8 teaspoon (0.5 g) salt

1/2 cup + 1 tablespoon (80 g) all-purpose flour

Preheat the oven to 400ºF (200ºC) for at least 15 to 20 minutes. The oven must be hot when you bake the cheesecake.

Lightly grease a 9-inch (23-cm) round springform pan. Then line with two overlapping sheets of parchment paper, making sure the parchment comes at least 2 inches (5 cm) above the pan's top on all sides. Don't worry if the paper doesn't look smooth; the cheesecake's outer sides should look rustic, so that's okay! Place the pan on a rimmed baking sheet.

Using an electric hand mixer or a stand mixer, beat the cream cheese on low speed for 2 to 3 minutes, until smooth and free of any lumps. Add the yogurt and sugar and continue mixing until incorporated.

Gradually add the sweetened condensed milk and beat until creamy, 1 to 2 minutes. Add the heavy cream, vanilla, milk powder, baking powder, and salt; beat on medium-high speed for 2 minutes.

Turn off the mixer and sift the flour evenly over the cream cheese mixture. Beat on low speed until incorporated, about 20 seconds. Scrape down the sides of the bowl and continue to beat until the batter is very smooth, homogenous, and silky, about 15 seconds.

Pour the batter into the prepared pan and tap gently on the counter to remove any air bubbles.

Bake for 45 to 55 minutes, or until deeply golden brown on top and still very jiggly in the center.

Let cool for 20 minutes. The center of the cheesecake will fall drastically, and that is what you want. Then remove the pan's sides. Let cool completely before carefully peeling away the parchment from the sides of the cheesecake and transferring it to a serving plate. Slice into wedges and serve at room temperature.

ORIANA'S NOTES:

This cheesecake can be made 1 to 2 days ahead. Store well covered in the refrigerator. Before serving, be sure to let the cheesecake sit at room temperature to remove the chill.

CUPCAKES

EGGLESS ULTIMATE CHOCOLATE CUPCAKES

There should be a permanent spot in your recipe box for these Eggless Ultimate Chocolate Cupcakes! These cupcakes are super chocolatey, moist, rich, and delicious. I've topped them with swirls of American Chocolate Buttercream here, but you can dress them with whatever your heart desires.

Makes 12 cupcakes

For the Eggless Ultimate Chocolate Cupcakes

1 cup (200 g) granulated sugar

3/4 cup (180 ml) buttermilk

4 tablespoons (60 g) unsalted butter, melted

1/4 cup (60 ml) vegetable oil

1/4 cup (60 g) sour cream

1 teaspoon (5 ml) pure vanilla extract

1 tablespoon (15 ml) hot water (optional)

1 teaspoon (1 g) instant espresso powder (optional)

1-1/4 cups (175 g) all-purpose flour

1/4 cup + 2 tablespoons (45 g) unsweetened natural cocoa powder

2 teaspoons (8 g) baking powder

1/4 teaspoon (1.5 g) baking soda

1/4 teaspoon (1 g) salt

To Decorate

1 batch American Chocolate Buttercream (page 145)

Mini chocolate crispearls to taste

Make the Eggless Ultimate Chocolate Cupcakes

Preheat the oven to 350ºF (180ºC). Line a 12-cup cupcake pan with cupcake liners.

Combine the sugar, buttermilk, melted butter, oil, sour cream, and vanilla extract in a large bowl and whisk together.

In a small bowl, combine the hot water and instant espresso powder, if using. Add to the butter mixture; mix to combine.

Add the flour, cocoa powder, baking powder, baking soda, and salt; stir until just combined.

Fill the cupcake liners about two-thirds full.

Bake for 18 to 22 minutes, or until a toothpick inserted in the center comes out clean. Cool in the pan on a wire rack for 5 minutes, and then remove the cupcakes from the pan. Place the cupcakes back on the rack, and cool to room temperature, about 1 hour, before frosting. Unfrosted cupcakes can be stored at room temperature for up to 3 days or frozen for up to 1 month; defrost at room temperature before decorating and serving. Take into consideration that the cupcakes will lose some of their fluffiness if refrigerated or frozen.

Decorate

Spread or pipe the buttercream evenly on the cupcakes. Sprinkle with mini chocolate crispearls and serve. The frosted cupcakes can be stored at room temperature for up to 1 day, or in the refrigerator for up to 3 days.

Scan with your phone for my **Eggless Vanilla Cupcake Recipe**

EGGLESS WHITE CHOCOLATE RASPBERRY CUPCAKES

These Eggless White Chocolate Raspberry Cupcakes are to die for! Not too sweet, not too rich—just simple perfection, through and through. Light and fluffy with a soft, tender crumb, they are filled with raspberry sauce and then dressed in a rich white chocolate buttercream. These are bound to be your new favorites.

Makes 12 cupcakes

For the Raspberry Sauce

2 teaspoons (10 ml) water, divided

1 teaspoon (4 g) cornstarch

1-1/2 cups (200 g) fresh or frozen raspberries

2 tablespoons (25 g) granulated sugar

For the Eggless White Chocolate Cupcakes

3/4 cup (180 ml) milk

1/2 cup (85 g) white chocolate chips or chunks

2 cups (280 g) all-purpose flour

2-1/2 teaspoons (10 g) baking powder

1/4 teaspoon (1.5 g) baking soda

1/2 teaspoon (2 g) salt

1/2 cup (115 g) unsalted butter, softened

1/2 cup (100 g) granulated sugar

2 tablespoons (30 g) sour cream

1 teaspoon (5 ml) apple cider vinegar

1 teaspoon (5 ml) pure vanilla extract

To Assemble and Decorate

1 batch American White Chocolate Buttercream (page 147)

Fresh raspberries (optional)

Make the Raspberry Sauce

Mix 1 teaspoon water with the cornstarch in a small bowl. Set aside.

Combine the raspberries, sugar, and remaining teaspoon of water in a small saucepan over medium heat. Stir the mixture, breaking up some of the raspberries as you stir. Once simmering, add the cornstarch mixture. Continue to stir and simmer for 3 to 4 minutes.

Remove the pan from the heat and press the raspberry sauce through a fine-mesh strainer to remove the seeds. Allow the raspberry sauce to cool completely before using. Cover and store for up to 1 week in the refrigerator.

Make the Eggless White Chocolate Cupcakes

Preheat the oven to 350ºF (180ºC). Line a 12-cup cupcake pan with cupcake liners.

Combine the milk and white chocolate in a microwave-safe mixing bowl or liquid measuring cup. Heat in the microwave in 30-second bursts, stirring between each burst, until smooth and melted. Set aside to cool.

Sift the flour, baking powder, baking soda, and salt together into a large bowl.

Using an electric hand mixer or a stand mixer, beat the butter on medium-high speed until pale and creamy, 3 to 4 minutes. Add the sugar and beat on high speed for 2 minutes until creamed and pale, scraping down the sides and up the bottom of the bowl with a rubber spatula as needed. Then add the sour cream, vinegar, and vanilla; continue beating to combine, about 1 minute.

Turn the mixer to low and add the flour mixture in three batches, alternating with the cooled milk-chocolate mixture, beginning and ending with the flour mixture. Beat until just combined, 30 to 45 seconds. Do not overmix.

Fill the cupcake liners about two-thirds full.

Bake for 18 to 22 minutes, or until a toothpick inserted in the center comes out clean. Cool in the pan on a wire rack for 5 minutes, and then remove the cupcakes from the pan. Place back on the rack, and cool to room temperature about 1 hour, before frosting. Unfrosted cupcakes can be stored at room temperature for up to 3 days or frozen for up to 1 month; defrost at room temperature before frosting and serving. Take into consideration that the cupcakes will lose some of their fluffiness if refrigerated or frozen.

Assemble and Decorate

Use a knife (or a cupcake corer) to carve a hollow in the center of each cupcake. Fill the center of each cupcake with raspberry sauce, and then place the carved piece back on top.

Spread or pipe the frosting evenly on the cupcakes.

Top the cupcakes with some fresh raspberries, if desired, and serve. The frosted cupcakes can be stored at room temperature for up to 1 day, or in the refrigerator for up to 3 days.

EGGLESS LEMON CUPCAKES

Lemon is one of my absolute favorite cupcake flavors. These Eggless Lemon Cupcakes are moist, sweet, buttery, and loaded with fresh lemon flavor! Plus, they're amazingly easy to make. Anytime I've brought these scrumptious cupcakes to a potluck or party, they've vanished within minutes, so you may want to bake a double batch.

Makes 12 cupcakes

For the Eggless Lemon Cupcakes

2 cups (280 g) all-purpose flour

2 teaspoons (8 g) baking powder

1/4 teaspoon (1.5 g) baking soda

1/4 teaspoon (1 g) salt

3/4 cup (180 ml) milk

1/4 cup (60 ml) fresh lemon juice

1/2 cup (115 g) unsalted butter, softened

1 cup (200 g) granulated sugar

1 teaspoon (5 ml) pure vanilla extract

1 tablespoon (8 g) lemon zest

To Assemble and Decorate

1 batch Lemon Buttercream (page 156)

Yellow sanding sugar (optional)

Lemon peel curls (optional)

Make the Eggless Lemon Cupcakes

Preheat the oven to 350ºF (180ºC). Line a 12-cup cupcake pan with cupcake liners.

Sift the flour, baking powder, baking soda, and salt together into a large bowl.

In a mixing bowl or liquid measuring cup, combine the milk and lemon juice.

Using an electric hand mixer or a stand mixer, beat the butter on medium-high speed until creamy, 3 to 4 minutes. Add the sugar and beat on high speed for 2 minutes, until creamed and pale, scraping down the sides and up the bottom of the bowl with a rubber spatula as needed. Then add the vanilla and lemon zest; continue beating to combine, about 1 minute.

Turn the mixer to low and add the flour mixture in three batches, alternating with the milk mixture, beginning and ending with the flour mixture. Beat until just combined, 30 to 45 seconds. Do not overmix.

Fill the cupcake liners about two-thirds full.

Bake for 18 to 22 minutes, or until a toothpick inserted in the center comes out clean. Cool in the pan on a wire rack for 5 minutes, and then remove the cupcakes from the pan. Place back on the rack, and cool to room temperature, about 1 hour, before frosting. Unfrosted cupcakes can be stored at room temperature for up to 3 days or frozen for up to 1 month; defrost at room temperature before frosting and serving. Take into consideration that the cupcakes will lose some of their fluffiness if refrigerated or frozen.

Decorate

Spread or pipe the lemon buttercream evenly on the cooled cupcakes. Sprinkle with yellow sanding sugar and top with a lemon peel curl, if desired. The frosted cupcakes can be stored at room temperature for up to 1 day, or in the refrigerator for up to 3 days.

Scan with your phone for my **Eggless Lemon Cake Recipe**

EGGLESS CANNOLI CUPCAKES

This recipe takes all those delicious cannoli flavors and turns them into a cupcake that you can easily make at home. These Cannoli Cupcakes have all the flavors of the traditional dessert. They're light and just a bit sweet, with a slight touch of cinnamon. The cannoli frosting is so good you'll want to eat it right out of the mixer bowl.

Makes 12 cupcakes

For the Eggless Cannoli Cupcakes

2 cups (280 g) all-purpose flour

2-1/2 teaspoons (10 g) baking powder

1/4 teaspoon (1.5 g) baking soda

1 teaspoon (3 g) ground cinnamon

1/4 teaspoon (1 g) salt

1 cup (240 ml) milk

1 tablespoon (15 ml) apple cider vinegar

1/2 cup (115 g) unsalted butter, softened

1 cup (200 g) granulated sugar

2 tablespoons (30 g) plain regular yogurt

2 teaspoons (10 g) pure vanilla extract

To Decorate

1 batch Cannoli Frosting (page 166)

Mini chocolate chips (optional)

Chopped pistachios (optional)

Make the Eggless Cannoli Cupcakes

Preheat the oven to 350ºF (180ºC). Line a 12-cup cupcake pan with cupcake liners.

Sift the flour, baking powder, baking soda, cinnamon, and salt together into a large bowl.

In a mixing bowl or liquid measuring cup, combine the milk and vinegar.

Using an electric hand mixer or a stand mixer, beat the butter on medium-high speed until creamy, 3 to 4 minutes. Add the sugar and beat on high speed for 2 minutes, until creamed and pale, scraping down the sides and up the bottom of the bowl with a rubber spatula as needed. Then add the yogurt and vanilla; continue beating to combine, about 1 minute.

Turn the mixer to low and add the flour mixture in three batches, alternating with the milk mixture, beginning and ending with the flour mixture. Beat until just combined, 30 to 45 seconds. Do not overmix.

Fill the cupcake liners about two-thirds full.

Bake for 18 to 22 minutes, or until a toothpick inserted in the center comes out clean. Cool in the pan on a wire rack for 5 minutes, and then remove the cupcakes from the pan. Place the cupcakes back on the rack, and cool to room temperature, about 1 hour, before frosting. Unfrosted cupcakes can be stored at room temperature for up to 3 days or frozen for up to 1 month; defrost at room temperature before frosting and serving. Take into consideration that the cupcakes will lose some of their fluffiness if refrigerated or frozen.

Assemble and Decorate

Use a knife (or a cupcake corer) to carve a hollow in the center of each cupcake.
Fill the center of each cupcake with cannoli frosting, and then place the carved piece back on top.

Spread or pipe more cannoli frosting evenly on the cupcakes, sprinkle with mini chocolate chips and pistachios, if desired, and serve. The frosted cupcakes can be stored at room temperature for up to 1 day, or in the refrigerator for up to 3 days.

EGGLESS CHOCOLATE CREAM CUPCAKES

Here is my homemade take on the Hostess cupcake! My daughter always wanted to try one of these, so I came out with this eggless version. They might not be exactly like the originals, but they do the trick. They take a little time to make but are well worth it. A creamy filling is piped into chocolate cupcakes with a pastry bag, and then the cupcakes are glazed with chocolate and decorated with more cream.

Makes 12 cupcakes

For the Eggless Chocolate Cream Cupcakes

1 cup (200 g) granulated sugar

3/4 cup (180 ml) buttermilk

4 tablespoons (60 g) unsalted butter, melted

1/4 cup (60 ml) vegetable oil

1/4 cup (60 g) sour cream

1 teaspoon (5 ml) pure vanilla extract

1 tablespoon (15 ml) hot water (optional)

1 teaspoon (1 g) instant espresso powder (optional)

1-1/4 cups (175 g) all-purpose flour

1/4 cup + 2 tablespoons (45 g) unsweetened natural cocoa powder

2 teaspoons (8 g) baking powder

1/4 teaspoon (1.5 g) baking soda

1/4 teaspoon (1 g) salt

For the Cream Filling

1 teaspoon (3 g) unflavored gelatin powder

3 tablespoons (45 ml) water

4 tablespoons (56 g) unsalted butter, softened

1 teaspoon (5 ml) pure vanilla extract

1/4 teaspoon (1 g) salt

1-1/4 cups (280 g) Eggless Marshmallow Crème (page 169)

For the Chocolate Glaze

1/2 cup (100 g) chocolate chips or chunks

3 tablespoons (42 g) unsalted butter

Make the Eggless Chocolate Cream Cupcakes

Preheat the oven to 350ºF (180ºC). Line a 12-cup cupcake pan with cupcake liners.

Combine the sugar, buttermilk, melted butter, oil, sour cream, and vanilla extract into a large bowl and whisk together.

In a small bowl, combine the hot water and instant espresso powder, if using. Add to the butter mixture; mix to combine.

Add the flour, cocoa powder, baking powder, baking soda, and salt; stir until just combined.

Fill the cupcake liners about two-thirds full.

Bake for 18 to 22 minutes, or until a toothpick inserted in the center comes out clean. Cool in the pan on wire racks for 5 minutes, and then remove the cupcakes from the pan. Place the cupcakes back on the rack, and cool to room temperature, about 1 hour, before frosting. Unfrosted cupcakes can be stored at room temperature for up to 3 days or frozen for up to 1 month; defrost at room temperature before decorating and serving. Take into consideration that the cupcakes will lose some of their fluffiness if refrigerated or frozen.

Make Cream Filling

Sprinkle the gelatin over the water in a bowl and let sit until the gelatin softens, about 5 minutes. Then microwave for 30 seconds to dissolve the gelatin. Whisk in the butter, vanilla, and salt until combined. Let the mixture cool until barely warm, about 5 minutes. Whisk in the marshmallow crème until smooth. Refrigerate the filling for at least 30 minutes and up to 2 days.

Make the Chocolate Glaze

Combine the chocolate and butter in a microwave-safe bowl and microwave at 50 percent power in 30-second bursts, stirring after each burst, until the chips have melted and the mixture is smooth. Let the glaze cool completely, about 10 minutes.

Assemble and Decorate

Use a knife (or a cupcake corer) to carve a hollow in the center of each cupcake.

Measure 1/4 cup of the filling and set aside to decorate the cupcakes. Use the remaining filling to fill the center of each cupcake, using about a tablespoon per cupcake. Place the carved pieces back on top, pressing to adhere.

Frost each cupcake with 2 teaspoons of the chocolate glaze. Transfer the reserved crème filling to a pastry bag, pipe curlicues across the tops of the glazed cupcakes, and serve. The frosted cupcakes can be stored at room temperature for up to 2 days, or in the refrigerator for up to 5 days.

EGGLESS SPRINKLE SURPRISE CUPCAKES

Colorful sprinkles inside the cupcakes will make your next party a big hit! My kids go nuts for anything with sprinkles on it, so Eggless Sprinkle Surprise Cupcakes are always a favorite. The surprise is a rainbow of colorful sprinkles that are hidden in the center of each cupcake. These cupcakes will bring a smile to all of your faces.

Makes 12 cupcakes

For the Eggless Sprinkle Surprise Cupcakes

2 cups (280 g) all-purpose flour

2-1/2 teaspoons (10 g) baking powder

1/4 teaspoon (1.5 g) baking soda

1/4 teaspoon (1 g) salt

1 cup (240 ml) milk

1 tablespoon (15 ml) apple cider vinegar

1/2 cup (115 g) unsalted butter, softened

1 cup (200 g) granulated sugar

2 tablespoons (30 g) sour cream

2 teaspoons (10 ml) pure vanilla extract

To Assemble and Decorate

1/2 cup (95 g) of your favorite sprinkles, for filling

1 small batch Eggless Vanilla Swiss Meringue Buttercream (page 152)

Gel food coloring

Make the Eggless Sprinkle Surprise Cupcakes

Preheat the oven to 350ºF (180ºC). Line a 12-cup cupcake pan with cupcake liners.

Sift the flour, baking powder, baking soda, and salt together into a large bowl.

In a mixing bowl or liquid measuring cup, combine the milk and vinegar.

Using an electric hand mixer or a stand mixer, beat the butter on medium-high speed until creamy, 3 to 4 minutes. Add the sugar and beat on high speed for 2 minutes, until creamed and pale, scraping down the sides and up the bottom of the bowl with a rubber spatula as needed. Then add the sour cream and vanilla; continue beating to combine, about 1 minute.

Turn the mixer to low and add the flour mixture in three batches, alternating with the milk mixture, beginning and ending with the flour mixture. Beat until just combined, 30 to 45 seconds. Do not overmix.

Fill the cupcake liners about two-thirds full.

Bake for 18 to 22 minutes, or until a toothpick inserted in the center comes out clean. Cool in the pan on a wire rack for 5 minutes, and then remove the cupcakes from the pan. Place the cupcakes back on the rack, and cool to room temperature, about 1 hour, before frosting. Unfrosted cupcakes can be stored at room temperature for up to 3 days.

Assemble and Decorate

Use a knife (or a cupcake corer) to carve a hollow in the center of each cupcake.

Fill the center of each cupcake with 1 teaspoon sprinkles, and then place the carved piece back on top.

Add enough gel food coloring to the buttercream to reach your desired color(s), and then spread or pipe the buttercream evenly on the cupcakes and serve. The frosted cupcakes can be stored at room temperature for up to 1 day, or in the refrigerator for up to 3 days.

ORIANA'S NOTES:

To decorate these cupcakes, I colored the buttercream with two colors. Then I placed the buttercream in two separate piping bags and inserted both bags into a large (16-inch / 40-cm) disposable piping bag fitted with a decorative tip. If you want to make the same decoration, make sure the two bags are aligned by squeezing and twisting the large bag. Then squeeze out a test pipe to ensure the colors are coming out evenly.

EGGLESS CARROT CUPCAKES

This recipe is a crowd-pleaser, made completely from scratch with real grated carrots. These cupcakes are soft, fluffy, and moist and are topped with an easy Maple Cinnamon Buttercream and chopped walnuts. They're perfect for Easter or anytime of year—now we can have our cake and eat our vegetables, too!

Makes 12 cupcakes

For the Eggless Carrot Cupcakes

1-1/2 cups (210 g) all-purpose flour

1-1/2 teaspoons (6 g) baking powder

1/4 teaspoon (1.5 g) baking soda

1 teaspoon (3 g) ground cinnamon

1/4 teaspoon (0.59 g) ground nutmeg

1/4 teaspoon (1 g) salt

1/2 cup (115 g) unsalted butter, softened

2/3 cup (134 g) brown sugar

1/3 cup (67 g) granulated sugar

1/4 cup (60 g) plain regular yogurt

1/4 cup (60 g) unsweetened applesauce

2 tablespoons (30 ml) milk

1 teaspoon (5 ml) pure vanilla extract

1 cup shredded (90 g) carrots

To Decorate

1 batch Maple Cinnamon Buttercream (page 158)

1/2 cup (60 g) chopped walnuts

Make the Eggless Carrot Cupcakes

Preheat the oven to 350ºF (180ºC). Line a 12-cup cupcake pan with cupcake liners.

Sift the flour, baking powder, baking soda, cinnamon, nutmeg, and salt together into a large bowl.

Using an electric hand mixer or a stand mixer, beat the butter on medium-high speed until creamy, 3 to 4 minutes. Add the sugars and beat on high speed for 2 minutes, until creamed and pale, scraping down the sides and up the bottom of the bowl with a rubber spatula as needed. Then add the yogurt, applesauce, milk, and vanilla; continue beating to combine, about 1 minute.

Turn the mixer to low and add the flour mixture; beat until just combined, 30 to 45 seconds. Do not overmix. Fold in the shredded carrots.

Fill the cupcake liners about two-thirds full.

Bake for 20 to 25 minutes, or until a toothpick inserted in the center comes out clean. Cool in the pan on a wire rack for 5 minutes, and then remove the cupcakes from the pan. Place the cupcakes back on the rack, and cool to room temperature, about 1 hour, before frosting. Unfrosted cupcakes can be stored at room temperature for up to 3 days or frozen for up to 1 month; defrost at room temperature before frosting and serving. Take into consideration that the cupcakes will lose some of their fluffiness if refrigerated or frozen.

Decorate

Spread or pipe the buttercream evenly on the cupcakes. Sprinkle with chopped walnuts and serve. The frosted cupcakes can be stored at room temperature for up to 1 day, or in the refrigerator for up to 3 days.

Scan with your phone for my **Eggless Carrot Bundt Cake Recipe**

ORIANA'S NOTES:

These cupcakes are also wonderful frosted with Cream Cheese Frosting (page 161).

EGGLESS STRAWBERRY CUPCAKES

These Eggless Strawberry Cupcakes are soft, light, and packed with real strawberry flavor! They're made from scratch with no artificial strawberry flavor, just pure strawberries. The secret is adding reduced fresh strawberry puree to the batter. This puree will add lots of strawberry flavor to your cupcakes without adding extra moisture, and it also contributes a lovely pink color. My family adores these cupcakes—they're strawberry heaven!

Makes 12 cupcakes

For the Eggless Strawberry Cupcakes

2 cups (280 g) all-purpose flour

2-1/2 teaspoons (10 g) baking powder

1/4 teaspoon (1.5 g) baking soda

1/4 teaspoon (1 g) salt

1 cup (240 ml) milk

1 tablespoon (15 ml) apple cider vinegar

1/2 cup (115 g) unsalted butter, softened

1 cup (200 g) granulated sugar

2 tablespoons (30 g) strawberry puree (see Strawberry Frosting recipe on page 163 for how to make strawberry puree)

1 teaspoon (5 ml) pure vanilla extract

To Decorate

1 batch Strawberry Frosting (page 163)

6 fresh strawberries, halved (optional)

Make the Eggless Strawberry Cupcakes

Preheat the oven to 350ºF (180ºC). Line a 12-cup cupcake pan with cupcake liners.

Sift the flour, baking powder, baking soda, and salt together into a large bowl.

In a mixing bowl or liquid measuring cup, combine the milk and vinegar.

Using an electric hand mixer or a stand mixer, beat the butter on medium-high speed until creamy, 3 to 4 minutes. Add the sugar and beat on high speed for 2 minutes, until creamed and pale, scraping down the sides and up the bottom of the bowl with a rubber spatula as needed. Then add the strawberry puree and vanilla; continue beating to combine, about 1 minute.

Turn the mixer to low and add the flour mixture in three batches, alternating with the milk mixture, beginning and ending with the flour mixture. Beat until just combined, 30 to 45 seconds. Do not overmix.

Fill the cupcake liners about two-thirds full.

Bake for 18 to 22 minutes, or until a toothpick inserted in the center comes out clean. Cool in the pan on a wire rack for 5 minutes, and then remove the cupcakes from the pan. Place the cupcakes back on the rack, and cool to room temperature, about 1 hour, before frosting. Unfrosted cupcakes can be stored at room temperature for up to 3 days or frozen for up to 1 month; defrost at room temperature before frosting and serving. Take into consideration that the cupcakes will lose some of their fluffiness if refrigerated or frozen.

Decorate

Spread or pipe the frosting evenly on the cupcakes. Top each cupcake with a strawberry half, if desired, and serve. The frosted cupcakes can be stored at room temperature for up to 1 day, or in the refrigerator for up to 3 days.

Scan with your phone to learn **how to make strawberry puree**

EGGLESS BANANA CUPCAKES

Banana is a flavor that people seem to either love or hate. If you are on the love side, as we are, this recipe is for you. I top these moist and dense, yet still soft, banana cupcakes with decadent Brown Sugar Buttercream and then sprinkle them with cinnamon sugar. You'll be buying extra bananas to make sure you have enough to make these dream banana cupcakes!

Makes 12 cupcakes

For the Eggless Banana Cupcakes

1-1/2 cups (210 g) all-purpose flour

2 teaspoons (8 g) baking powder

1/4 teaspoon (1.5 g) baking soda

1 teaspoon (3 g) ground cinnamon

1/4 teaspoon (1 g) salt

1/2 cup (120 ml) milk

1-1/2 teaspoons (7.5 ml) apple cider vinegar

1/2 cup (115 g) unsalted butter, softened

1/2 cup (100 g) granulated sugar

1/4 cup (50 g) brown sugar

1 large (120 g) ripe banana, mashed

1/4 cup (60 g) plain regular yogurt

1 teaspoon (5 ml) pure vanilla extract

To Decorate

1 batch Brown Sugar Buttercream (page 157)

Cinnamon sugar (see note)

Make the Eggless Banana Cupcakes

Preheat the oven to 350ºF (180ºC). Line a 12-cup cupcake pan with cupcake liners.

Sift the flour, baking powder, baking soda, cinnamon, and salt together into a large bowl.

In a mixing bowl or liquid measuring cup, combine the milk and vinegar. Let the mixture rest for 5 to 8 minutes, until thickened and curdled.

Using an electric hand mixer or a stand mixer, beat the butter on medium-high speed until creamy, 3 to 4 minutes. Add the sugars and beat on high speed for 2 minutes, until creamed and pale, scraping down the sides and up the bottom of the bowl with a rubber spatula as needed. Then add the mashed banana, yogurt, and vanilla; continue beating to combine, about 1 minute.

Turn the mixer to low and add the flour mixture in three batches, alternating with the milk mixture, beginning and ending with the flour mixture. Beat until just combined, 30 to 45 seconds. Do not overmix.

Fill the cupcake liners about two-thirds full.

Bake for 18 to 22 minutes, or until a toothpick inserted in the center comes out clean. Cool in the pan on a wire rack for 5 minutes, and then remove the cupcakes from the pan. Place the cupcakes back on the rack, and cool to room temperature, about 1 hour, before frosting. Unfrosted cupcakes can be stored at room temperature for up to 3 days or frozen for up to 1 month; defrost at room temperature before frosting and serving. Take into consideration that the cupcakes will lose some of their fluffiness if refrigerated or frozen.

Decorate

Spread or pipe the buttercream evenly on the cupcakes. Sprinkle with cinnamon sugar and serve. The frosted cupcakes can be stored at room temperature for up to 1 day, or in the refrigerator for up to 3 days.

ORIANA'S NOTES:

To make cinnamon sugar, simply mix 2 tablespoons granulated sugar with 1 teaspoon ground cinnamon, or a little more or less to taste.

EGGLESS MINI VANILLA BEAN CUPCAKES

These Eggless Mini Vanilla Bean Cupcakes make the perfect little bite-sized treats for children's parties, weddings, or birthday celebrations. They are easy to hold and lower in sugar and fat. They are totally customizable; you can use any frosting you want, add sprinkles, fill them with jam—the possibilities are endless. Sometimes smaller is better, so let's make some mini cupcakes!

Makes 48 mini cupcakes

For the Eggless Mini Vanilla Bean Cupcakes

2 cups (280 g) all-purpose flour

2-1/2 teaspoons (10 g) baking powder

1/4 teaspoon (1.5 g) baking soda

1/4 teaspoon (1 g) salt

1 cup (240 ml) milk

1 tablespoon (15 ml) apple cider vinegar

1/2 cup (115 g) unsalted butter, softened

1 cup (200 g) granulated sugar

2 vanilla beans

2 tablespoons (30 g) plain yogurt

1 teaspoon (5 ml) pure vanilla extract

To Decorate

1 small batch Eggless Vanilla Swiss Meringue Buttercream (page 152)

Make the Eggless Mini Vanilla Bean Cupcakes

Preheat the oven to 350ºF (180ºC). Line two 24-cup mini cupcake pans with mini cupcake liners.

Sift the flour, baking powder, baking soda, and salt together into a large bowl.

In a mixing bowl or liquid measuring cup, combine the milk and vinegar.

Using an electric hand mixer or a stand mixer, beat the butter on medium-high speed until creamy, 3 to 4 minutes. Add the sugar and beat on high speed for 2 minutes, until creamed and pale, scraping down the sides and up the bottom of the bowl with a rubber spatula as needed. Split the vanilla beans and scrape the seeds into the creamed mixture; discard the beans. Then add the yogurt and vanilla extract; continue beating to combine, about 1 minute.

Turn the mixer to low and add the flour mixture in three batches, alternating with the milk mixture, beginning and ending with the flour mixture. Beat until just combined, 30 to 45 seconds. Do not overmix.

Fill the cupcake liners about two-thirds full.

Bake for 15 to 18 minutes, or until a toothpick inserted in the center comes out clean. Cool in the pans on wire racks for 5 minutes, and then remove the cupcakes from the pans. Place the cupcakes back on the racks, and cool to room temperature, about 1 hour, before frosting. Unfrosted cupcakes can be stored at room temperature for up to 3 days or frozen for up to 1 month; defrost at room temperature before frosting and serving. Take into consideration that the cupcakes will lose some of their fluffiness if refrigerated or frozen.

Decorate

Spread or pipe the vanilla buttercream evenly on the cupcakes and serve. The frosted cupcakes can be stored at room temperature for up to 1 day, or in the refrigerator for up to 3 days.

BREAD & MUFFINS

EGGLESS CARAMEL-GLAZED APPLE BREAD

Here's a lovely Eggless Caramel-Glazed Apple Bread that will give you all the fall feels. It's chock-full of tart apples with a generous caramel glaze. This apple bread has the best flavor and an almost pound cake–like texture. You won't be able to stop eating it. It's effortless to make, makes your kitchen smell amazing, and stores well, as it keeps moist for days. Be sure to wait until the bread is completely cool before slicing.

Makes one 8-1/2 x 4-1/2 inch (23.5 x 12.7 cm) loaf

2 cups (280 g) all-purpose flour

1 tablespoon (12 g) baking powder

1 teaspoon (6 g) baking soda

2 teaspoons (4 g) apple pie spice

1/2 teaspoon (2 g) salt

1/2 cup (115 g) unsalted butter, melted

2/3 cup (120 g) brown sugar

1/2 cup (120 ml) maple syrup

1/4 cup (60 g) applesauce

1/4 cup (60 ml) buttermilk

2 teaspoons (10 ml) pure vanilla extract

2 cups (240 g) chopped, peeled apples
  (about 2 medium-size apples)

1/2 cup (120 ml) Salted Caramel
  (page 166)

Adjust the oven rack to the lower-middle position. Preheat the oven to 325ºF (165ºC). Grease an 8-1/2 x 4-1/2 inch (23.5 x 12.7 cm) loaf pan with nonstick baking spray with flour.

In a medium bowl, whisk the flour, baking powder, baking soda, apple pie spice, and salt together. Set aside.

In a medium mixing bowl, combine the melted butter and brown sugar; mix until the sugar is dissolved. Add the maple syrup, applesauce, buttermilk, and vanilla; mix until combined.

Fold the chopped apples into the batter thoroughly.

Pour the mixture into the prepared loaf pan.

Bake for 45 to 50 minutes, or until a toothpick inserted in the center comes out clean.

Cool in the pan on a wire rack for 15 minutes, and then remove the loaf from the pan and set on the wire rack to cool completely.

Once cooled, drizzle with the salted caramel. Serve warm or at room temperature. Store in an airtight container for up to 4 days at room temperature or in the refrigerator for up to a week.

Scan with your phone for my **Eggless Apple Cake Recipe**

ORIANA'S TIPS:

The apples can be shredded instead of chopped, if desired.

If you don't have apple pie spice, you can substitute 1 teaspoon ground cinnamon, 1/2 teaspoon ground nutmeg, 1/4 teaspoon ground allspice, and 1/4 teaspoon ground ginger.

EGGLESS CARROT BANANA MUFFINS

My kid only eats carrots if they are hidden inside a cupcake, cake, or muffin. I know, it's sad, but it's my reality. As a result, you'll find me hiding vegetables in my baked goods very often. These Eggless Carrot Banana Muffins are always a hit and disappear in a flash! They're soft, fluffy, and oh-so-perfectly moist with lots of texture, yet they're still light. They'll be your family's next favorite.

Makes 8 muffins

1-1/2 cups (210 g) all-purpose flour

1-1/2 teaspoons (6 g) baking powder

1/2 teaspoon (3 g) baking soda

1/2 teaspoon (1 g) ground cinnamon

1/4 teaspoon (0.5 g) ground nutmeg

1/4 teaspoon (1 g) salt

1/2 cup (240 ml) milk

2 teaspoons (10 ml) apple cider vinegar

1/2 cup (115 g) unsalted butter, softened

1/2 cup (100 g) granulated sugar

1/4 cup (50 g) brown sugar

3/4 cup (120 g) ripe mashed banana

1/4 cup (60 g) plain yogurt

1 teaspoon (5 ml) pure vanilla extract

1 cup (85 g) freshly grated carrot

1/4 cup (28 g) old-fashioned rolled oats

Preheat the oven to 425ºF (220ºC). Spray 8 cavities of the muffin pan with nonstick spray or line with cupcake liners.

Whisk the flour, baking powder, baking soda, cinnamon, nutmeg, and salt together in a large bowl until combined.

In a mixing bowl or liquid measuring cup, combine the milk and vinegar. Let the mixture rest for 5 to 8 minutes, until thickened and curdled.

Using an electric hand mixer or a stand mixer, beat the butter on medium-high speed until creamy and pale, 3 to 4 minutes. Add the sugars and beat on high speed for 2 minutes until creamed, scraping down the sides and up the bottom of the bowl with a rubber spatula as needed. Then add the mashed banana, yogurt, and vanilla; continue beating to combine, about 1 minute.

Turn the mixer to low and add the flour mixture in three batches, alternating with the milk mixture, beginning and ending with the flour mixture. Beat until just combined, 30 to 45 seconds. Do not overmix. Fold in the grated carrot.

Spoon the batter evenly into eight muffin cups or liners, filling each one all the way to the top. Top with the rolled oats.

Bake for 5 minutes, and then reduce the oven temperature to 375ºF (190ºC). Continue baking until golden brown and a toothpick inserted in the center comes out clean, another 15 to 20 minutes.

Allow the muffins to cool for 5 minutes in the muffin pan, and then transfer to a wire rack to continue cooling. Store at room temperature for up to 3 days or in the refrigerator for up to 1 week.

EGGLESS LEMON POPPY SEED LOAF

This Eggless Lemon Poppy Seed Loaf is rich, buttery, and perfectly moist and tender. It's packed with delicious lemony flavors with a delicate hint of aromatic lavender, and drizzled with just the right lemon-sugar glaze. Easy to bake, it makes for a great breakfast, teatime snack, or dessert, with or without the glaze.

Makes one 8-1/2 x 4-1/2 inch (235 x 127 cm) loaf

For the Eggless Lemon Poppy

Seed Loaf

2 cups (280 g) all-purpose flour
2 teaspoons (8 g) baking powder
1/4 teaspoon (1.5 g) baking soda
1/4 teaspoon (1 g) salt
1 tablespoon (12 g) poppy seeds
3/4 cup (180 ml) milk
1 tablespoon (8 g) lemon zest
1/2 teaspoon (1 g) culinary lavender
1/4 cup (60 ml) fresh lemon juice
1 teaspoon (5 ml) pure vanilla extract
1/2 cup (115 g) unsalted butter, softened
1 cup (200 g) granulated sugar

For the Lemon-Sugar Glaze

1 cup (120 g) confectioners' sugar, sifted
1 tablespoon (15 ml) lemon juice
1 tablespoon (15 ml) heavy cream or milk

Make the Eggless Lemon Poppy Seed Loaf

Adjust the oven rack to the middle position and preheat the oven to 350°F (180°C). Grease and flour an 8-1/2 x 4-1/2 inch (235 x 127 cm) loaf pan. You can also use a nonstick baking spray with flour.

Sift the flour, baking powder, baking soda, and salt together into a large bowl. Add the poppy seeds and mix to combine. Set aside.

Place the milk in a microwave-safe cup or bowl and microwave for 40 to 60 seconds, until warm to the touch. Sprinkle in the lemon zest and lavender and let it infuse for 5 minutes. Add the lemon juice and vanilla extract; mix to combine. Set aside.

Using an electric hand mixer or a stand mixer, beat the butter on medium-high speed until creamy, 3 to 4 minutes. Add the granulated sugar and beat on high speed for 2 minutes, until creamed and pale, scraping down the sides and up the bottom of the bowl with a rubber spatula as needed. Then add the milk mixture; continue beating to combine, about 1 minute.

Reduce the mixer speed to low, add the flour mixture, and beat just to combine. Do not overmix. Scrape down the mixing bowl with a spatula and turn the batter over several times to ensure all of the ingredients are well incorporated.

Pour the mixture into the prepared pan, using a spatula to spread it if necessary.

Bake for 35 to 40 minutes, or until a toothpick inserted in the center comes out clean. Allow the loaf cake to cool for 10 minutes in the pan, and then remove from the pan and let cool completely on a wire rack. The cake must be completely cool before glazing.

Make the Lemon-Sugar Glaze

Whisk all the glaze ingredients together and pour over the loaf cake. Let the glaze set for 5 minutes. Serve. Store in an airtight container for up to 4 days at room temperature or in the refrigerator for up to a week.

EGGLESS DOUBLE CHOCOLATE MUFFINS

Better-than-bakery chocolate muffins! These Eggless Double Chocolate Muffins are made entirely from scratch using cocoa powder and chocolate chips. Super chocolatey, moist, and dense, these have everything you'd want in a muffin, including crunchy tops and a to-die-for chocolate flavor. You won't need any other recipe.

Makes 8 muffins

3/4 cup (105 g) all-purpose flour

1/2 cup (60 g) whole-wheat flour

1 cup (200 g) granulated sugar

1/4 cup + 2 tablespoons (45 g) unsweetened natural cocoa powder

2 teaspoons (8 g) baking powder

1/4 teaspoon (1.5 g) baking soda

1/4 teaspoon (1 g) salt

1 tablespoon (15 ml) hot water (optional)

1 teaspoon (1 g) instant espresso powder (optional)

3/4 cup (180 ml) buttermilk

4 tablespoons (56 g) unsalted butter, melted

1/4 cup (60 ml) vegetable or canola oil

1/4 cup (60 g) sour cream

1 teaspoon (5 ml) pure vanilla extract

1/2 cup (100 g) semisweet chocolate chips

Preheat the oven to 425°F (220°C). Spray 8 cavities of the muffin pan with nonstick spray or line with cupcake liners.

Whisk the flours, sugar, cocoa powder, baking powder, baking soda, and salt together in a large bowl until combined.

In a mixing bowl, combine the hot water and espresso powder, if using. Add the buttermilk, melted butter, oil, sour cream, and vanilla; mix until well combined.

Fold the wet ingredients into the dry ingredients and mix everything together by hand. Do not overmix. Stir in the chocolate chips.

Spoon the batter evenly into the 8 muffin cups or liners, filling each one all the way to the top.

Bake for 5 minutes, and then reduce the oven temperature to 375°F (190°C). Continue baking until golden brown and a toothpick inserted in the center comes out clean, another 20 to 25 minutes.

Allow the muffins to cool for 5 minutes in the pan, and then transfer to a wire rack to continue cooling. Store at room temperature for up to 3 days, and then transfer to the refrigerator for up to 1 week.

EGGLESS CRUMB BANANA BREAD

This Eggless Crumb Banana Bread is delicious and moist, with the same wonderful flavors of a traditional banana bread, topped off with cinnamon crumble for the ultimate treat. The recipe is straightforward, and you most likely have all the ingredients in your pantry already. It's our favorite bread to share with family, friends, and neighbors. There is nothing better than receiving a warm loaf of banana bread—except receiving a warm loaf of banana bread that has a cinnamon crumb topping!

Makes one 8-1/2 x 4-1/2 inch (235 x 127 cm) loaf

For the Crumb

1/2 cup + 2 tablespoons (88 g) all-purpose flour

1/2 cup (100 g) granulated sugar

1/2 teaspoon (1 g) ground cinnamon

1/8 teaspoon (0.5 g) salt

1/4 cup (58 g) unsalted butter, melted

For the Eggless Crumb Banana Bread

3 ripe bananas (about 270 g)

1/2 cup (115 g) unsalted butter, melted

1/2 cup (120 ml) buttermilk

2 teaspoons (10 ml) pure vanilla extract

1 cup (100 g) brown sugar

1-1/2 cups (210 g) all-purpose flour

1 teaspoon (2 g) ground cinnamon

1 teaspoon (4 g) baking powder

1/2 teaspoon (3 g) baking soda

1/4 teaspoon (1 g) salt

Make the Crumb

In a small bowl, mix all the crumb ingredients together with a fork until crumbly; set aside.

Make the Eggless Crumb Banana Bread

Adjust the oven rack to the middle position and preheat the oven to 350°F (180°C). Grease and flour an 8-1/2 x 4-1/2 inch (235 x 127 cm) loaf pan. You can also use a nonstick baking spray with flour.

In a medium bowl, mash the ripe bananas with a fork until completely smooth.

Stir the melted butter into the mashed bananas; mix until combined. Add the buttermilk, vanilla, and brown sugar; mix to combine.

Mix in the flour, cinnamon, baking powder, baking soda, and salt until combined.

Pour the mixture into the prepared loaf pan. Sprinkle the crumb topping evenly over the batter.

Bake for 1 hour or until a wooden pick comes out clean.

Cool in the pan for 5 minutes, and then transfer to a wire rack. Serve warm or at room temperature. Store in an airtight container for up to 4 days at room temperature or in the refrigerator for up to a week.

ORIANA'S NOTES:

The bananas must be very ripe (soft and darkly speckled). If your bananas are not ripe enough, you can bake them at 350°F (180°C) for 8 to 10 minutes and then use them as instructed in the recipe.

For extra yumminess, add 1-1/4 cups toasted walnuts after adding the dry ingredients.

EGGLESS DULCE DE LECHE–STUFFED DONUT MUFFINS

They may look like muffins, but a dunk in melted butter and a roll in cinnamon sugar make these baked treats taste like your favorite sugared donut. Hidden inside each muffin is a delicious dulce de leche filling. Perfect for breakfast, brunch, snack, or even as a dessert.

Makes 8 muffins

For the Eggless Dulce de Leche–Stuffed Donut Muffins

1 cup (140 g) all-purpose flour

1/2 cup (60 g) whole-wheat flour

1/2 cup (100 g) granulated sugar

2 teaspoons (8 g) baking powder

1/4 teaspoon (1.5 g) baking soda

1/2 teaspoon (2 g) salt

1/2 teaspoon (1 g) ground cinnamon

1/4 teaspoon (0.5 g) ground nutmeg (optional)

1 cup (240 ml) buttermilk

6 tablespoons (84 g) unsalted butter, melted

2 tablespoons (30 ml) vegetable oil

1 teaspoon (5 ml) pure vanilla extract

8 teaspoons (160 g) dulce de leche

For the Cinnamon-Sugar Topping

1/4 cup (50 g) granulated sugar

2 teaspoons (4 g) ground cinnamon

3 tablespoons (45 g) unsalted butter

Make the Eggless Dulce de Leche–Stuffed Donut Muffins

Preheat the oven to 425°F (220°C). Spray 8 cavities of the muffin pan with nonstick spray or line with cupcake liners.

Whisk the flours, sugar, baking powder, baking soda, salt, cinnamon, and nutmeg together in a large bowl until combined.

In a mixing bowl, combine the buttermilk, melted butter, oil, and vanilla.

Fold the wet ingredients into the dry ingredients and mix everything together by hand. Do not overmix; the batter will be thick and a little lumpy.

Spoon 1 heaping tablespoon of batter into each muffin cup or liner. Add 1 teaspoon dulce de leche in the center of the batter, and then spoon another heaping tablespoon of batter on top of the dulce the leche. Repeat until you complete 8 muffins.

Bake for 5 minutes, and then reduce the oven temperature to 375°F (190°C). Continue baking until golden brown and a toothpick inserted in the center comes out clean, another 15 to 20 minutes.

Allow the muffins to cool for 5 minutes in the muffin pan, and then transfer to a wire rack to continue cooling for 10 more minutes.

Make the Cinnamon-Sugar Topping

In a small bowl, mix together the sugar and cinnamon.

In another small bowl, melt the butter.

After the muffins have cooled slightly, dip each one into the melted butter, and then roll in the cinnamon-sugar mixture. Store the muffins in an airtight container for up to 5 days.

ORIANA'S NOTES:

You can substitute Nutella or Biscoff spread for the dulce de leche.

EGGLESS PUMPKIN CHOCOLATE CHIP BREAD

If you only make one eggless pumpkin bread in your life, this is the recipe you need. This recipe is packed with pumpkin flavor and tons of chocolate chips. It's soft, dense, and totally delicious. Sweet enough to fit into the dessert category, but humble enough for breakfast or brunch, it's perfect to have on hand for coffee, snack time, and unexpected guests.

Makes one 8-1/2 x 4-1/2 inch (235 x 127 cm) loaf

2 cups (280 g) all-purpose flour

1 tablespoon (6 g) pumpkin pie spice

2 teaspoons (8 g) baking powder

1/4 teaspoon (1.5 g) baking soda

1 teaspoon (4 g) salt

1 cup (200 g) brown sugar

1/3 cup (67 g) granulated sugar

1/2 cup (115 g) unsalted butter, melted

10 ounces (283 g) pumpkin puree

1/3 cup (80 g) plain yogurt or sour cream

1/3 cup (80 g) applesauce

3 tablespoons (45 ml) vegetable or canola oil

2/3 cup (133 g) semisweet chocolate chips

Adjust the oven rack to the lower-middle position. Preheat the oven to 325ºF (165ºC). Grease an 8-1/2 x 4-1/2 inch (235 x 127 cm) loaf pan with nonstick baking spray with flour.

In a medium bowl, whisk together the flour, pumpkin pie spice. baking powder, baking soda, and salt. Set aside.

In another medium mixing bowl, combine the sugars and melted butter; mix until the sugars are dissolved. Add the pumpkin puree, yogurt, applesauce, and oil; mix until combined.

Fold the chocolate chips into the batter thoroughly.

Pour the mixture into the prepared loaf pan. Top with more chocolate chips, if desired.

Bake for 50 to 60 minutes, or until a toothpick inserted in the center comes out clean.

Cool the bread in the pan on a wire rack for 15 minutes, and then remove the loaf from the pan and continue to cool on the wire rack. Store at room temperature for up to 3 days, and then transfer to the refrigerator for up to 1 week.

> **ORIANA'S NOTES:**
>
> Instead of 1 tablespoon pumpkin pie spice, you can use 2 teaspoons ground cinnamon, 1/2 teaspoon ground ginger, 1/4 teaspoon ground cloves, and 1/4 teaspoon ground nutmeg.

EGGLESS JUMBO BLUEBERRY STREUSEL MUFFINS

These sky-high, soft, and tender Eggless Jumbo Blueberry Streusel Muffins have that bakery-style look. But they taste better because they're homemade; after all, homemade is always better. Each bite is moist and exploding with juicy blueberries. The batter comes together quickly, making these the perfect treat to whip up any morning of the week.

Makes 6 jumbo muffins

For the Streusel Topping

1/2 cup (70 g) all-purpose flour

1/2 cup (100 g) granulated sugar

1/8 teaspoon (0.5 g) salt

1/4 cup (58 g) unsalted butter, melted

For the Eggless Jumbo Blueberry Muffins

2 cups (280 g) all-purpose flour

1/2 cup (100 g) granulated sugar

1 tablespoon (12 g) baking powder

1/4 teaspoon (1.5 g) baking soda

1/2 teaspoon (2 g) salt

1 cup (170 g) blueberries

1-1/2 cups (360 ml) buttermilk

4 tablespoons (57 grams) unsalted butter, melted and cooled

1 teaspoon (5 ml) apple cider vinegar

1 teaspoon (5 ml) vanilla extract

Sugar glaze to drizzle (optional) (page 169)

Make the Streusel Topping

In a small bowl, mix all the topping ingredients together with a fork until crumbly; set aside.

Make the Eggless Jumbo Blueberry Muffins

Preheat the oven to 425ºF (220ºC). Spray a 6-cup jumbo muffin pan with nonstick spray or line with cupcake liners.

Whisk the flour, sugar, baking powder, baking soda, and salt together in a large bowl until combined. Add the blueberries and mix to coat with the flour mixture.

In a mixing bowl, combine the buttermilk, melted butter, vinegar, and vanilla.

Fold the wet ingredients into the dry ingredients and mix everything together by hand. Do not overmix; the batter will be thick and a little lumpy.

Fill the muffin cups right to the top, and sprinkle with the streusel mixture.

Bake for 5 minutes, and then reduce the oven temperature to 375ºF (190ºC). Continue baking until golden brown and a toothpick inserted in the center comes out clean, another 20 to 25 minutes.

Allow the muffins to cool for 5 minutes in the muffin pan, and then transfer to a wire rack to continue cooling. Drizzle the cooled muffins with sugar glaze, if desired. Store covered at room temperature for 3 to 4 days, and then transfer to the refrigerator for up to 1 week.

ORIANA'S TIPS:

You can use fresh or frozen blueberries to make this recipe. If using frozen blueberries, do not thaw.

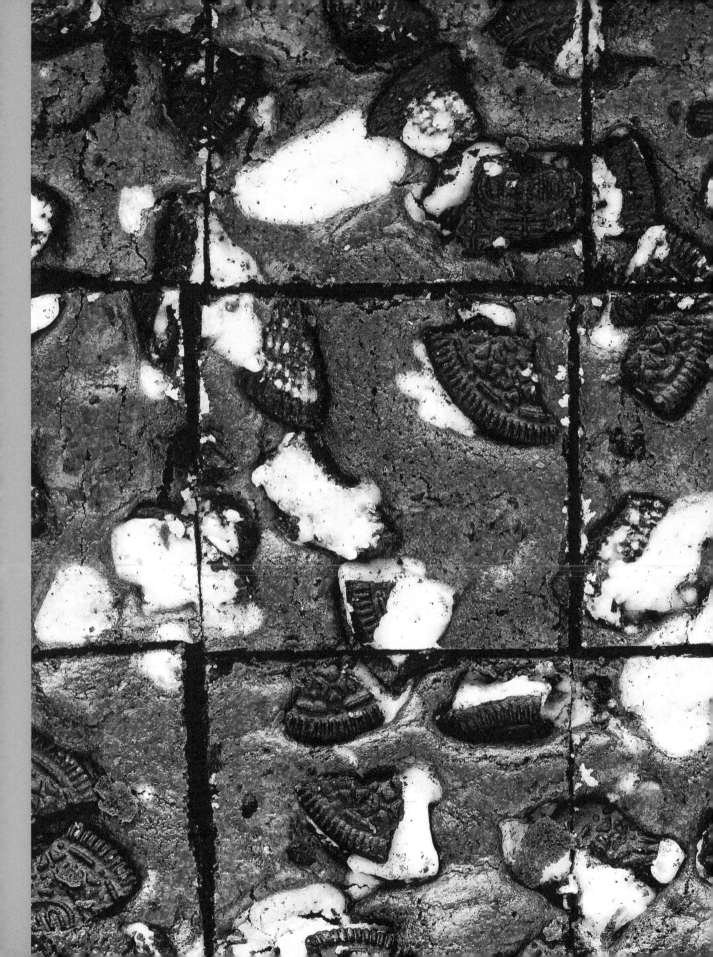

BROWNIES & BARS

EGGLESS SLUTTY BROWNIES

Slutty Brownies are the most decadent and outrageous bar cookie you'll ever try! Layers of cookie dough, Oreos, and homemade brownie batter—they're sinfully delicious. One small bite will be enough to satisfy any sweet tooth, but trust me, you won't stop there!

Makes 9 brownies

For the Eggless Cookie Dough

1-1/4 cups (175 g) all-purpose flour

1/4 teaspoon (1.5 g) baking soda

1/4 teaspoon (1 g) baking powder

1/2 teaspoon (2 g) salt

1/2 cup (115 g) unsalted butter, softened

1/4 cup + 2 tablespoons (75 g) granulated sugar

1/4 cup + 2 tablespoons (75 g) brown sugar

1 tablespoon + 1-1/2 teaspoons (22.5 ml) milk

1/2 teaspoon (2.5 ml) pure vanilla extract

3/4 cup (150 g) semisweet chocolate chips or chunks

For the Cookie Layer

16 Oreo cookies

For the Eggless Brownie Layer

1/2 cup (115 g) unsalted butter, melted

1/2 cup (100 g) granulated sugar

1/2 cup (100 g) brown sugar

1/2 teaspoon (0.5 g) instant espresso powder (optional)

1 teaspoon (5 ml) pure vanilla extract

1/4 cup + 1 tablespoon (38 g) unsweetened natural cocoa powder

3/4 cup (105 g) all-purpose flour

1 teaspoon (4 g) baking powder

1/8 teaspoon (0.75 g) baking soda

1/4 cup + 2 tablespoons (90 ml) buttermilk

1/2 cup (100 g) semisweet chocolate chips or chocolate chunks

Make the Eggless Cookie Dough

Preheat the oven to 350ºF (180ºC). Line an 8 x 8 x 3 inch (20 x 20 x 7.5 cm) square baking pan with parchment paper. The parchment paper should extend above the walls of the baking pan to allow for easy removal at the end. Lightly grease with baking spray.

Combine the flour, baking soda, baking powder, and salt in a bowl. Set aside.

Using an electric hand mixer or a stand mixer, beat the butter and sugars on medium speed until smooth and creamy, 3 to 4 minutes. Scrape down the sides and bottom of the bowl as needed. Add the milk and vanilla; mix until incorporated.

Reduce the speed to low, and then gradually beat in the flour mixture until combined. Stir in the chocolate chips and mix until evenly distributed.

Spread the dough in an even layer on the bottom of the prepared pan.

Make the Cookie Layer

Place the Oreos on top of the cookie dough layer; breaking the cookies to fit as needed. Set aside while making the brownie layer.

Make the Eggless Brownie Layer

Combine the butter, granulated sugar, and brown sugar in a large microwave-safe bowl. Microwave for 30 seconds, and then remove and stir with a whisk. Repeat this process 2 to 3 more times until the mixture looks glossy and the butter is completely melted. Allow the mixture to cool slightly.

Add the espresso powder, if using, and the vanilla extract; mix until well incorporated. Add the cocoa powder and continue mixing until incorporated.

Add half of the flour, the baking powder, and the baking soda; mix until combined. Add the buttermilk and mix until combined. Add the remaining flour and mix until just combined. Fold in the chocolate chips. Do not overmix the batter.

Spread the batter over the Oreo layer. If desired, add more chopped Oreos on top.

Bake for 45 to 50 minutes, or until a toothpick inserted in the center comes out with just a few moist crumbs attached. Transfer the pan to a wire rack and cool completely, about 4 hours, before cutting.

Lift the brownies out of the pan using the parchment overhang. Use a large serrated knife to cut the slutty brownies into thirds crosswise and lengthwise. Store at room temperature for up to 3 days.

> **ORIANA'S NOTES:**
>
> If you use a glass baking dish instead of a metal baking pan, let the brownies cool for 10 minutes and then remove them from the pan; otherwise, the heat retained by the glass can lead to overbaking.

EGGLESS CHOCOLATE CHIP COOKIE BARS

These Eggless Chocolate Chip Cookie Bars are soft and chewy on the inside with a slightly crunchy outside. Taste testers gave these chocolate chip cookie bars a stamp of approval. They're incredibly easy to make. You don't have to chill the cookie dough, and you don't need to roll the dough into individual cookies. You can easily scale the recipe up for a crowd or make this ahead for an amazing on-demand treat. Sprinkle with sea salt for a little something extra.

Makes 12 to 16 bars

2-1/2 cups (350 g) all-purpose flour
1 teaspoon (6 g) baking soda
1 teaspoon (4 g) salt
1 cup (230 g) unsalted butter, softened
3/4 cup (150 g) granulated sugar
3/4 cup (150 g) brown sugar
3 tablespoons (45 ml) milk
1 teaspoon (5 ml) apple cider vinegar
1 teaspoon (5 ml) pure vanilla extract
1 cup (200 g) semisweet chocolate chips
Sea salt flakes (optional)

Preheat the oven to 350ºF (180ºC). Line a 9 x 13 inch (24 x 35 cm) baking pan with parchment paper and lightly spray with baking spray. The parchment paper should extend above the walls of the baking pan to allow for easy removal at the end.

Combine the flour, baking soda, and salt in a bowl. Set aside.

Using an electric hand mixer or a stand mixer, beat the butter and sugars on medium speed until smooth and creamy, 3 to 4 minutes. Scrape down the sides and bottom of the bowl as needed. Add the milk, vinegar, and vanilla; mix until incorporated.

Reduce the speed to low, and then gradually beat in the flour mixture until combined. Stir in the chocolate chips and mix until evenly distributed.

Scrape the mixture into the prepared pan and spread into an even layer. Top with more chocolate chips and sprinkle with sea salt flakes, if desired.

Bake for 25 to 30 minutes, or until a toothpick inserted in the middle comes out clean.

Allow the bars to cool completely in the pan. Once cool, lift the parchment paper out of the pan using the overhang on the sides, and then cut into small bars. Store in an airtight container at room temperature for up to a week.

Scan with your phone for
my **Eggless Chocolate
Chip Skillet Cookie Recipe**

EGGLESS WHITE CHOCOLATE BLONDIES

Blondies are basically the first cousin to brownies! While they may look a little pale, I promise you, they can hold their own against their chocolate counterparts. These Eggless White Chocolate Blondies are soft, moist, and delightfully buttery with a subtle caramel flavor, allowing the taste of white chocolate to shine through. We especially love these blondies for how easy they are to make.

Makes 16 blondies

1-1/2 cups (210 g) all-purpose flour

1/2 teaspoon (2 g) baking powder

1/4 teaspoon (1.5 g) baking soda

1/4 teaspoon (1 g) salt

4 tablespoons (58 g) unsalted butter, melted

3/4 cup (150 g) brown sugar

1/4 cup (50 g) granulated sugar

1/2 cup (120 ml) milk

1/4 cup (50 g) unsweetened applesauce

1 tablespoon (15 ml) pure vanilla extract

1 cup (200 g) white chocolate chips

Preheat the oven to 350°F (175°C). Line the bottom and sides of a 9 x 13 inch (24 x 35 cm) baking pan with aluminum foil, leaving enough overhang on all sides of the baking pan to allow for easy removal at the end. Set aside.

In a medium bowl, stir together the flour, baking powder, baking soda, and salt. Set aside.

In a large bowl, stir the melted butter and sugars together until combined. Add the milk, applesauce, and vanilla.

Gently fold the dry ingredients into the wet ingredients. Be careful not to overmix; the batter will be thick. Fold in the white chocolate chips.

Spread the dough in an even layer on the bottom of the prepared pan.

Bake for 20 to 22 minutes, or until a toothpick inserted in the center comes out with just a few moist crumbs attached. Transfer the pan to a wire rack and cool completely, about 4 hours, before cutting.

Lift the foil out of the pan using the overhang on the sides and cut into bars. Store at room temperature for up to 3 days.

ORIANA'S NOTES:

These blondies are perfect to eat on their own, or you can eat them warm with a scoop of vanilla ice cream and a drizzle of Salted Caramel (page 166).

EGGLESS MINT CHOCOLATE BROWNIES

Brownies are one of my go-to desserts, and these Eggless Mint Chocolate Brownies are a family favorite! Indulge in a classic bar with three delicious layers—fudgy brownies, minty filling, and chocolate glaze. They're moist, thick, fudgy, and exactly what a brownie should be. The perfect treat for parties and get-togethers. Warning: They'll be gone in seconds!

Makes 9 brownies

For the Eggless Brownie Layer

1/2 cup (115 g) unsalted butter, melted

1/2 cup (100 g) granulated sugar

1/2 cup (100 g) brown sugar

1 teaspoon (5 ml) pure vanilla extract

1/2 teaspoon (0.5 g) instant espresso powder (optional)

1/4 cup + 1 tablespoon (38 g) unsweetened natural cocoa powder

3/4 cup (105 g) all-purpose flour

1 teaspoon (4 g) baking powder

1/8 teaspoon (0.75 g) baking soda

1/4 cup + 2 tablespoons (90 ml) buttermilk

1/2 cup (100 g) semisweet chocolate chips or chocolate chunks

For the Mint Frosting Layer

1/2 cup (115 g) unsalted butter, softened

2 cups (240 g) confectioners' sugar

2 tablespoons (30 ml) milk

1-1/4 teaspoons (8.75 ml) peppermint extract

1/4 teaspoon (1 g) salt

1 to 2 drops gel green food coloring

For the Chocolate Layer

4 tablespoons (58 g) unsalted butter

1/2 cup (100 g) semisweet chocolate chips

Make the Eggless Brownie Layer

Preheat the oven to 350ºF (180ºC). Line an 8 x 8 x 3 inch (20 x 20 x 7.5 cm) square baking pan with parchment paper. The parchment paper should extend above the walls of the baking pan to allow easy removal at the end. Lightly spray with baking spray.

Combine the butter and sugars in a large microwave-safe bowl. Microwave for 30 seconds, and then remove and stir with a whisk. Repeat this process 2 to 3 more times until the mixture looks glossy and the butter is completely melted. Allow the mixture to cool slightly.

Combine the vanilla extract and espresso powder, if using; mix until well incorporated. Add the cocoa powder and continue mixing until incorporated.

Add half of the flour, the baking powder, and the baking soda; mix until combined. Add the buttermilk; mix until combined. Add the remaining flour and mix until just combined. Do not overmix the batter.

Fold in the chocolate chips.

Scrape the batter into the prepared pan. Bake for 25 to 30 minutes, or until a toothpick inserted halfway between the edge and the center comes out with just a few moist crumbs attached. Transfer the pan to a wire rack and cool in the pan for 1-1/2 hours.

Once completely cooled, lift the parchment paper out of the pan using the overhang on the sides. Place the brownies on a baking sheet as you make the frosting.

Make the Mint Frosting Layer

In a large bowl, using an electric hand mixer or a stand mixer, beat the butter on medium speed until smooth and creamy, 3 to 4 minutes.

Reduce the mixer speed to low, add 1 cup of the confectioners' sugar, and mix until incorporated. Add the milk, peppermint extract, salt, and food coloring. Once incorporated, add the remaining confectioners' sugar; beat on low speed for 1 minute, and then increase the speed to medium-high and beat for 4 to 5 minutes, until the frosting is smooth, fluffy, and spreadable, scraping down the bowl once or twice.

Frost the cooled brownies with the frosting and refrigerate for at least 1 hour. This allows the frosting to "set" on top of the brownies, which makes spreading the chocolate layer easy.

Make the Chocolate Layer

Melt the butter and chocolate chips in a medium saucepan over medium heat, stirring constantly, about 5 minutes. Or melt in the microwave in 20-second increments, stirring after each.

Once melted and smooth, pour the chocolate over the mint layer. Gently spread with a knife or offset spatula. Place the brownies in the refrigerator and chill for 1 hour to set the chocolate.

Once chilled, remove from the refrigerator and cut into squares. Store in the refrigerator for up to 5 days.

ORIANA'S NOTES:

Use a sharp knife to cut the brownies. For extra-neat squares, wipe the knife clean between each cut.

EGGLESS STRAWBERRY CRUMB BARS

These Eggless Strawberry Crumb Bars are totally irresistible; the bars are relatively easy to make and pack big flavor. A buttery crumb topping goes on the bottom and the top of these bars. It's like a strawberry crumb sandwich, which would be my favorite kind of sandwich! They're the type of bars that are perfect with a cup of coffee in the afternoon or a scoop of ice cream for an easy dessert.

Makes 9 bars

For the Eggless Strawberry Crumb Bars

2-1/2 cups (350 g) all-purpose flour

2/3 cup (134 g) granulated sugar

1/2 teaspoon (2 g) salt

1 cup + 2 tablespoons (259 g) unsalted butter, cold and cubed

1 teaspoon (5 ml) pure vanilla extract

1/2 cup (55 g) old-fashioned rolled oats

1/2 cup (63 g) pecans, toasted and chopped

1/4 cup (50 g) brown sugar

For the Strawberry Filling

2-1/2 cups (310 g) fresh strawberries, chopped

1/4 cup (50 g) granulated sugar

2 tablespoons (20 g) cornstarch

1 teaspoon (3 g) lemon zest

Make the Eggless Strawberry Crumb Bars

Adjust the oven rack to the middle position and heat the oven to 375ºF (190ºC).

Line an 8 x 8 inch (20 x 20 cm) square pan with parchment paper. The parchment paper should extend above the walls of the baking pan to allow for easy removal at the end. Lightly grease with baking spray.

Using an electric hand mixer or a stand mixer, whisk the flour, sugar, and salt together in a bowl. Beat in 1 cup of the butter, 1 tablespoon at a time, and the vanilla extract and continue mixing until the mixture resembles damp sand, about 2 minutes. Set aside 1-1/2 cups of the mixture for topping.

Sprinkle the remaining flour mixture into the prepared pan and press firmly into an even layer. Bake for 15 to 18 minutes, or until the edges of the crust begin to brown.

Meanwhile, stir the oats, pecans, and brown sugar into the reserved topping mixture. Add the remaining 2 tablespoons butter and pinch the mixture between your fingers into clumps. Set aside.

Make the Strawberry Filling

Gently mix all the filling ingredients together in a bowl.

Spread the strawberry mixture evenly over the hot crust, and then sprinkle with the reserved crumb topping. With the back of a large spoon or flat spatula, lightly press the topping down on the strawberry layer.

Bake for 22 to 25 minutes, or until the filling is bubbling and the topping is golden brown.

Let the bars cool completely in the pan on a wire rack, about 2 hours. Use the paper overhang to remove the bars from the pan. Cut into 9 pieces. Store in the refrigerator for up to 3 days.

ORIANA'S NOTES:

These crumb bars are best eaten the day they are baked, but they can be kept in an airtight container for up to 3 days (the crust and crumb will soften slightly with storage).

FUDGY EGGLESS CHOCOLATE BROWNIES

Nothing beats a homemade fudgy brownie—especially a brownie that is made in only one bowl. These Fudgy Eggless Chocolate Brownies are moist, dense, and rich. When you are having a chocolate emergency (yes, that is a real thing), these to-die-for eggless brownies are just what the doctor ordered.

Makes 9 brownies

1 cup (230 g) unsalted butter, melted

1 cup (200 g) granulated sugar

1 cup (200 g) brown sugar

1 tablespoon (15 ml) pure vanilla extract

1 teaspoon (1 g) instant espresso powder

3/4 cup (75 g) unsweetened natural cocoa powder

1-1/2 cups (210 g) all-purpose flour

2 teaspoons (8 g) baking powder

1/4 teaspoon (1.5 g) baking soda

3/4 cup (180 ml) buttermilk

1-1/2 cups (300 g) semisweet chocolate chips or chocolate chunks

Preheat the oven to 350ºF (180ºC). Line an 8 x 8 x 3 inch (20 x 20 x 7.5 cm) square baking pan with parchment paper. The parchment paper should extend above the walls of the baking pan to allow for easy removal at the end. Lightly grease with baking spray.

Combine the butter, granulated sugar, and brown sugar in a large microwave-safe bowl. Microwave for 30 seconds, and then remove and stir with a whisk. Repeat the process 2 to 3 more times until the mixture looks glossy and the butter is completely melted. Allow the mixture to cool slightly.

Add the vanilla extract and espresso powder; mix until well incorporated. Add the cocoa powder and continue mixing until incorporated.

Add half of the flour, the baking powder, and the baking soda; mix until combined. Add the buttermilk; mix until combined. Add the remaining flour and mix until just combined. Do not overmix the batter.

Fold in the chocolate chips.

Scrape the batter into the prepared pan. Bake for 40 to 50 minutes, or until a toothpick inserted halfway between the edge and the center comes out with just a few moist crumbs attached. Transfer the pan to a wire rack and let cool completely before cutting, about 1-1/2 hours.

Use the paper overhang to remove the bars from the pan. Use a large serrated knife to cut brownies into 9 pieces. Store at room temperature for up to 3 days.

ORIANA'S NOTES:

For thinner brownies, use a rectangular 9 x 13 inch (24 x 35 cm) baking pan.

EGGLESS RASPBERRY CHEESECAKE BARS

You will love these Eggless Raspberry Cheesecake Bars, with their crumbly crust and creamy, luscious filling. The creamiest cheesecake is swirled with fresh raspberry sauce and a sweet graham cracker crust. If you're wondering if it is as insanely delicious as it sounds, the answer is yes. This recipe is less intimidating than making a regular cheesecake—no need for a springform pan and no water bath.

Makes 9 bars

For the Raspberry Sauce

2 teaspoons (10 ml) water, divided

1 teaspoon (5 g) cornstarch

1-1/2 cups (200 g) fresh or frozen raspberries

2 tablespoons (25 g) granulated sugar

For the Crust

1-3/4 cups (175 g) graham cracker crumbs (from about 27 graham cracker squares)

5 tablespoons (75 g) unsalted butter, melted

2 tablespoons (25 g) granulated sugar

For the Eggless Cheesecake Filling

1-1/2 tablespoons (15 g) cornstarch

1-1/2 tablespoons (22.5 ml) water

12 ounces (340 g) full-fat cream cheese, softened

1/4 cup (50 g) granulated sugar

1/4 cup (60 g) full-fat sour cream

7 ounces (199 g) sweetened condensed milk

1/4 cup (60 ml) heavy cream, chilled

1-1/2 tablespoons (22.5 ml) fresh lemon juice

1 teaspoon (5 ml) pure vanilla extract

Scan with your phone for my **Eggless Mini Cheesecakes Recipe**

ORIANA'S NOTES:

Make sure to scrape the paddle and the sides of the bowl regularly when making the filling in order to achieve a silky, smooth texture.

Make the Raspberry Sauce

Mix 1 teaspoon of the water with the cornstarch in a small bowl. Set aside.

Combine the raspberries, sugar, and remaining teaspoon of water in a small saucepan over medium heat. Stir the mixture, breaking up some of the raspberries as you stir. Once simmering, add the cornstarch mixture. Continue to stir and simmer for 3 to 4 minutes.

Remove the pan from the heat and press the raspberry sauce through a fine-mesh strainer to remove the seeds. Allow the raspberry sauce to cool completely before using. Cover and store for up to 1 week in the refrigerator.

Make the Crust

Adjust the oven rack to the middle position and preheat the oven to 350ºF (180ºC). Line an 8 x 8 inch (20 x 20 cm) square pan with parchment paper. The parchment paper should extend above the walls of the baking pan to allow for easy removal at the end. Lightly grease with baking spray.

In a mixing bowl, combine the graham cracker crumbs, butter, and sugar with a fork until evenly moistened.

Firmly press the crumbs down onto the bottom of the prepared pan.

Bake for 5 to 8 minutes, or until the crust is fragrant and beginning to brown. Remove from the oven and prepare the filling.

Make the Eggless Cheesecake Filling

Mix the cornstarch and water in a small bowl until smooth. Set aside.

Using an electric hand mixer or a stand mixer, beat the cream cheese on low speed for 2 to 3 minutes, until smooth and free of any lumps. Add the sugar and sour cream and continue mixing until creamy and well incorporated. Gradually add the sweetened condensed milk, scraping down the bowl as necessary, and continue beating for 2 minutes. Add the heavy cream, lemon juice, vanilla extract, and cornstarch mixture; beat on high speed until well incorporated.

Pour the batter over the baked crust and spread into an even layer. Spoon small dollops of raspberry sauce over the cheesecake filling (add as much or as little as you like), then use a toothpick or knife tip to gently swirl everything together.

Bake for 30 to 35 minutes, or until the edges are set and the centers only slightly jiggle.

Set the pan on a wire rack and allow to cool at room temperature for 2 hours, and then transfer to the refrigerator and chill for at least 3 hours or up to 24 hours.

To slice, use the parchment overhang to lift the bars out of the pan as a whole, and then cut into squares with a sharp knife. For extra-neat squares, wipe the knife clean between each cut.

Cover and store leftover cheesecake bars in the refrigerator for up to 5 days.

EGGLESS DARK CHOCOLATE CHEESECAKE BARS

These Eggless Dark Chocolate Cheesecake Bars are indulgently rich and creamy! They feature an Oreo cookie crust, creamy chocolate cheesecake filling, chocolate ganache, and salted caramel—so decadent and a chocolate-lover's dream come true. These bars are an easy, fully make-ahead dessert that everyone will love!

Makes 9 bars

For the Crust

1-1/2 cups (195 g) Oreo crumbs (from 24 to 26 Oreos)

4 tablespoons (56 g) unsalted butter, melted

1 tablespoon (8 g) confectioners' sugar

For the Eggless Cheesecake Filling

3 tablespoons (30 g) cornstarch

3 tablespoons (45 ml) water

3/4 cup (180 ml) heavy cream

1 cup (180 g) semisweet chocolate chips

1 teaspoon (1 g) instant espresso powder

24 ounces (678 g) full-fat cream cheese

1/2 cup (100 g) granulated sugar

1/4 cup (25 g) natural unsweetened cocoa powder

1 14-ounce (397 g) can sweetened condensed milk

1 teaspoon (5 ml) pure vanilla extract

For the Chocolate Topping

1/2 cup (115 g) unsalted butter

1 cup (200 g) semisweet chocolate chips

1 teaspoon (3 g) sea salt flakes (optional)

ORIANA'S NOTES:

The cheesecake bars usually have a lip around the border since the center slightly sinks down, so it's easy to spread the chocolate topping, stopping around the border lip.

Drizzle these cheesecake bars with Salted Caramel (page 166) just before serving for an ultimate to-die-for dessert.

Make the Crust

Preheat the oven to 350°F (180°C). Lightly grease an 8 x 8 inch (20 x 20 cm) square pan and line with parchment paper. The parchment paper should extend above the walls of the baking pan to allow for easy removal at the end.

In a medium mixing bowl, combine the Oreo crumbs, melted butter, and confectioners' sugar. Pat the mixture firmly onto the bottom of the prepared pan.

Bake the crust for 8 to 10 minutes, or until the crust is fragrant and set. Place the pan on a wire rack and cool the crust completely. Leave the oven on.

Make the Eggless Cheesecake Filling

Mix the cornstarch and water in a small bowl until combined. Set aside.

Combine the heavy cream and chocolate chips in a small microwave-safe bowl or cup. Heat in 30-second bursts, stirring after each burst, until the chips have melted and the mixture is smooth. Stir in the espresso powder and set the mixture aside.

Using an electric hand mixer or a stand mixer, beat the cream cheese on low speed for 2 to 3 minutes, until smooth and free of any lumps. Add the sugar and cocoa powder; continue mixing until incorporated. Gradually add the sweetened condensed milk and beat until creamy, 1 to 2 minutes. Add the vanilla extract and cornstarch mixture; beat until well incorporated.

Add the melted chocolate mixture and beat until well incorporated.

Pour the mixture over the crust; tap gently on the counter to remove any air bubbles.

Bake for 40 minutes, or until the edges are just barely puffed. The center of the cheesecake bars should still wobble when you remove them from the oven. Set the pan on a rack to cool.

When completely cool, cover the pan and refrigerate for at least 6 hours, or ideally overnight.

Make the Chocolate Topping

Combine the butter and chocolate chips in a small microwave-safe bowl or cup. Heat in 30-second bursts, stirring after each burst, until the chips have melted and the mixture is smooth. Let the mixture cool for 2 to 3 minutes, and then pour and spread evenly over the chilled cheesecake bars. Sprinkle with sea salt, if desired.

Refrigerate the cheesecake bars for 30 minutes, or until the chocolate topping is set.

Loosen the cheesecake bars from the sides of the pan by running a thin metal spatula or knife around the inside rim. Using the parchment overhang, remove the cheesecake bars from the pan. Cut into 9 pieces. Cover and store cheesecake bars in the refrigerator for up to 5 days.

COOKIES

BEST EGGLESS SUGAR COOKIES

This is my favorite sugar cookie recipe because it turns out tender, buttery cookies that keep their shape when baked and taste amazing, too. With a flat surface for decorating, these stay soft for days and freeze beautifully. They're fun to make with kids around the holidays or anytime you need your cookie fix. Use your favorite cookie cutters and scan the QR code below to try my eggless royal icing!

Makes about 24 4-inch (10-cm) cookies

3 cups (420 g) all-purpose flour

1/2 teaspoon (2 g) baking powder

1/2 teaspoon (2 g) salt

3/4 cup (175 g) unsalted butter, softened

1 cup (200 g) granulated sugar

6 ounces (170 g) cream cheese, softened

2 teaspoons (10 ml) pure vanilla extract

Sift the flour and baking powder into a bowl. Add the salt and set aside.

Using an electric hand mixer or a stand mixer, beat the butter and sugar on medium speed until smooth and creamy, 3 to 4 minutes. Scrape down the sides and bottom of the bowl as needed. Add the cream cheese and vanilla; mix until incorporated.

Reduce the speed to low and gradually beat in the flour mixture; beat just until incorporated and the dough starts to come together. Divide the dough into two equal pieces.

Place one piece of dough on a big, lightly floured piece of parchment paper (or a silicone mat). With a lightly floured rolling pin, roll the dough out to about 1/4 to 1/8 inch (6 to 3 mm) thick. Lightly dust the rolled-out dough with flour. Place a piece of parchment on top to prevent sticking. Repeat with the second piece of dough.

Place both rolled-out doughs, one on top of the other, on a baking tray. Cover with plastic wrap or aluminum foil, and refrigerate for at least 2 hours and up to 2 days.

Preheat the oven to 350ºF (180ºC). Line two baking sheets with parchment paper or silicone baking mats.

Working with one sheet of dough at a time, use a cookie cutter to cut the dough into shapes. Transfer the shapes to the prepared baking sheets, spacing them about 1/2 inch apart. Gather up the dough scraps and form them into a disk, and then roll out and refrigerate for 15 to 20 minutes.

Bake for 10 to 13 minutes or until the cookies are just beginning to turn brown around the edges. Remove from the oven and let them sit on the baking sheets for 5 minutes. Then use a wide metal spatula to transfer the cookies to a wire rack and let cool completely. Repeat the process to cut and bake the remaining dough.

Decorate the cooled sugar cookies as desired. If using eggless royal icing, let the icing dry completely, about 1-1/2 hours, before serving. Once the cookies have completely dried, they can be stored either in an airtight container with waxed paper in between each layer, or in an airtight bag in a single layer. You can store them at room temperature for up to 1 week.

Scan with your phone to learn **how to make eggless royal icing**

ORIANA'S NOTES:

These eggless sugar cookies can be baked several weeks ahead and frozen. Just stack them up in a freezer bag and pop them in the freezer. When you're ready to serve, let them thaw at room temperature on a wire rack and then decorate.

ULTIMATE EGGLESS CHOCOLATE CHIP COOKIES

Chocolate chip cookies are a timeless classic dessert staple and an unbeatable comfort food. Serve warm, cold, or dunked in milk—no one can resist a good chocolate chip cookie. And with a slightly crispy outside and wonderfully soft and chewy inside, my eggless version is heaven for anyone.

Makes 36 cookies

2-1/2 cups (350 g) all-purpose flour

1/2 teaspoon (3 g) baking soda

1/2 teaspoon (2 g) baking powder

1 teaspoon (4 g) salt

1 cup (230 g) unsalted butter, softened

3/4 cup (150 g) granulated sugar

3/4 cup (150 g) packed brown sugar

3 tablespoons (45 ml) milk

1 teaspoon (5 ml) pure vanilla extract

2 cups (400 g) semisweet chocolate chips or chunks

Combine the flour, baking soda, baking powder, and salt in a bowl. Set aside.

Using an electric hand mixer or a stand mixer, beat the butter, granulated sugar, and brown sugar on medium speed until smooth and creamy, 3 to 4 minutes. Scrape down the sides and bottom of the bowl as needed. Add the milk and vanilla; mix until incorporated.

Reduce the speed to low and gradually beat in flour mixture; mix until combined. Stir in the chocolate chips and mix until evenly distributed.

Scoop out about 1-1/2 to 2 tablespoons of dough for each cookie. Roll each portion into a ball and place on a baking sheet or large plate. Freeze for at least 90 minutes or up to 2 days.

Preheat the oven to 350ºF (180ºC). Line two large baking sheets with parchment paper or silicone baking mats.

Place the frozen cookie balls on the prepared baking sheets, evenly spacing them about 2 inches apart. I recommend baking one sheet at a time.

Bake for 12 to 14 minutes, until barely golden brown around the edges, but still soft in the middle. When you remove the cookies from the oven, they will still look doughy and that's okay; they will continue to set as they cool.

Cool on the baking sheets for 5 minutes, and then transfer to wire racks to cool completely. Store in an airtight container at room temperature for up to a week.

ORIANA'S NOTES:

It's totally normal for some cookies to look misshapen after baking; if that happens, simply grab a spoon and shape the cookies by pressing the edges into the center. Do this as soon as they come out of the oven while they're still hot and moldable.

Right when the cookies come out of the oven, I like to press a couple of extra chocolate chips into the tops of the warm cookies. This is totally optional, but it makes the cookies extra chocolatey! I also like to sprinkle a few sea salt flakes over the top of each cookie.

EGGLESS BUTTER COOKIES

Butter cookies are one of those classic cookies that everyone loves. This eggless version is far better than what you'll find in tins at the store, in my humble opinion. I love the simple flavors and perfect crumb of these cookies. Make lovely designs with a large piping tip and dip in chocolate and sprinkles for a fun touch! They keep well, so they're perfect for gifting, and they're such a pretty cookie.

Makes 24 cookies

For the Eggless Butter Cookies

1 cup (230 g) unsalted butter, softened

1/2 cup (100 g) granulated sugar

1/4 cup + 1 tablespoon (75 g) cream cheese, softened

2 teaspoons (10 ml) pure vanilla extract (or ¼ teaspoon almond extract)

1/2 teaspoon (2 g) salt

2-1/2 cups (350 g) all-purpose flour

4 to 6 tablespoons (60 to 90 ml) milk

To Decorate (optional)

4 ounces (113 g) semisweet chocolate chips

1 tablespoon (14 g) butter

1/2 cup (95 g) sprinkles

Make the Eggless Butter Cookies

Using an electric hand mixer or a stand mixer, cream the butter and sugar on medium speed until light and fluffy, about 5 minutes. Add the cream cheese, vanilla, and salt, and mix until well incorporated. Scrape down the sides and bottom of the bowl as needed.

Reduce the speed to low and gradually beat in the flour; mix until just barely combined.

On medium speed, beat in 4 tablespoons of milk. You want a dough that's creamy and pipable, but still thick. If the dough is not pipable enough, add more milk 1 tablespoon at a time (you may need up to 6 tablespoons of milk in all).

Line two baking sheets with parchment paper or silicone baking mats.

Fill a piping bag fitted with a large star tip with the dough. Pipe the dough in 1 to 2 inch (3 to 5 cm) swirls 2 inches apart on the baking sheets. Chill the shaped cookies on the baking sheets for 20 to 30 minutes.

Preheat the oven to 400ºF (200ºC).

Bake the chilled cookies, one sheet at a time, for 10 to 12 minutes or until lightly browned on the sides. The cookies will spread but not completely lose their shape.

Remove from the oven and allow to cool on the baking sheets for 3 to 5 minutes. Then transfer to a wire rack to cool completely.

Decorate (optional)

Combine the chocolate and butter in a microwave-safe mixing bowl or liquid measuring cup. Heat in the microwave in 30-second bursts, stirring between each burst, until smooth and melted.

Dip half of each cooled cookie into the melted chocolate and top with sprinkles. Allow the chocolate to set completely at room temperature for about 1 hour or in the refrigerator for 20 minutes.

Store plain cookies in an airtight container at room temperature for up to 1 week. Cookies with chocolate should be stored in an airtight container at room temperature for 3 days or in the refrigerator for up to 1 week.

EGGLESS OATMEAL SCOTCHIES COOKIES

Oatmeal Scotchies are a classic oatmeal cookie full of butterscotch chips. These Eggless Oatmeal Scotchies Cookies are incredibly soft, chewy, packed with butterscotch chips, and easy to make, too. The perfect cookie for any occasion, they'll disappear from your cookie jar in no time.

Makes 16 big cookies

1-1/4 cups (175 g) all-purpose flour

1/2 teaspoon (2 g) baking powder

1/2 teaspoon (3 g) baking soda

1 teaspoon (2 g) ground cinnamon

1/2 teaspoon (2 g) salt

3/4 cup (170 g) unsalted butter, softened

1/2 cup (100 g) granulated sugar

1/2 cup (100 g) brown sugar

3 tablespoons (45 ml) milk

1 teaspoon (5 ml) pure vanilla extract

1-1/2 cups (150 g) old-fashioned rolled oats

1-1/4 cups (220 g) butterscotch chips

Combine the flour, baking powder, baking soda, cinnamon, and salt in a bowl. Set aside.

Using an electric hand mixer or a stand mixer, beat the butter, sugar, and brown sugar on medium speed until smooth and creamy, 3 to 4 minutes. Scrape down the sides and bottom of the bowl as needed. Add the milk and vanilla; mix until incorporated.

Reduce the speed to low and gradually beat in the flour mixture; mix until combined. Stir in the oats and butterscotch chips; mix until evenly distributed.

Scoop out 1-1/2 to 2 tablespoons of dough for each cookie. Roll each portion into a ball and place on a baking sheet or large plate. Freeze for at least 90 minutes or up to 2 days.

Preheat the oven to 350°F (180°C). Line two large baking sheets with parchment paper or silicone baking mats.

Place the frozen cookie balls on the prepared baking sheets, evenly spacing them about 2 inches apart. I recommend baking one sheet at a time.

Bake for 12 to 14 minutes, until barely golden brown around the edges, but still soft in the middle. When you remove the cookies from the oven, they will still look doughy and that's okay; they will continue to set as they cool.

Cool on the baking sheets for 5 minutes, and then transfer to wire racks to cool completely. Store in an airtight container at room temperature for up to a week.

ORIANA'S NOTES:

Right when the cookies come out of the oven, I like to press a couple of extra butterscotch chips into the tops of the warm cookies. This is totally optional but makes the cookies extra pretty!

SLICE-AND-BAKE EGGLESS LEMON COOKIES

For the true lemon lover, these Slice-and-Bake Eggless Lemon Cookies are the perfect treat! While I love all my cookie recipes, these lemon cookies are a family favorite. Every bite melts in your mouth, and the cookies themselves are basically foolproof. They're soft, tender, and packed with bold lemon flavor, with a deliciously light crumb. By the way, these cookies stay super soft for days.

Makes 18 cookies

1-1/2 cups (210 g) all-purpose flour

1/2 teaspoon (2 g) baking powder

1/4 teaspoon (1 g) salt

1/2 cup (115 g) unsalted butter, softened

1/2 cup (60 g) confectioners' sugar

2 tablespoons (30 g) cream cheese, softened

1 tablespoon (8 g) lemon zest, grated

1 teaspoon (5 ml) fresh lemon juice

1/4 cup (50 g) coarse sugar, for rolling

Whisk the flour, baking powder, and salt together in a medium bowl and set aside.

Using an electric hand mixer or a stand mixer, cream the butter and sugar on medium speed until light and fluffy, about 3 minutes. Add the cream cheese, lemon zest, and lemon juice and beat until combined. Scrape down the sides and bottom of the bowl as needed.

Add the dry ingredients to the butter mixture, and then mix on low until combined.

Put the coarse sugar in a long, shallow pan.

Shape the dough into a log about 10 inches (25 cm) long and roll gently in the coarse sugar to thoroughly coat. Wrap the log with plastic wrap and refrigerate for at least 2 hours or up to a month.

Preheat the oven to 350ºF (180ºC). Line two rimmed baking sheets with parchment paper or silicone baking mats.

Using a sharp knife, cut the log into 1/4-inch (6 mm) thick slices. Arrange the slices on the prepared baking sheets, spacing them about 1 inch apart.

Bake for 10 to 12 minutes, or until very lightly browned on the edges and slightly puffy. Let the cookies cool on the baking sheets for 5 minutes, and then transfer to a wire rack to cool completely. When cool, store layered between sheets of waxed paper in airtight containers for up to a week, or freeze for up to 3 months.

EGGLESS CARAMEL-STUFFED BROWNIE COOKIES

The beauty of Eggless Caramel-Stuffed Brownie Cookies is that you actually get a buttery chocolate cookie with a surprise filling. Each cookie tastes like a brownie with a fudgy center because, during the baking process, the caramel melts and turns into a gooey puddle in the middle of the cookie. Sweet, salty, and fudgy goodness—it really doesn't get much better!

Makes 14 cookies

1-1/4 cup (175 g) all-purpose flour

1/2 cup (50 g) natural unsweetened cocoa powder

1/2 teaspoon (2 g) baking powder

1/4 teaspoon (1 g) salt

1/2 cup (115 g) unsalted butter, cold and cubed

1/2 cup (100 g) granulated sugar

1/2 cup (100 g) brown sugar

3/4 cup (150 g) chocolate chips

3 tablespoons (45 ml) milk

1 teaspoon (5 ml) pure vanilla extract

14 chocolate-coated caramel candies

Sea salt flakes (optional)

Whisk the flour, cocoa, baking powder, and salt together in a medium bowl and set aside.

Using an electric hand mixer or a stand mixer, beat the cold butter on medium speed for 30 to 45 seconds just to break it down a little. Add the granulated sugar and brown sugar and mix until just combined, 30 to 45 seconds. Scrape down the sides and bottom of the bowl as needed.

Add the chocolate chips and mix to evenly distribute.

Reduce the speed to low and add the flour mixture; mix until it resembles coarse crumbs. Add the milk and vanilla; mix until the dough comes together into a big ball.

Scoop 2-tablespoon portions of the dough and roll into balls. Make a deep, wide hollow in each ball. Insert 1 caramel candy in the middle, and then close up the dough over the candy and roll back into a ball. Make sure to seal the sides so the caramel is securely stuffed inside. Repeat to form 14 cookies. Freeze for at least 2 hours and up to 2 months.

Preheat the oven to 350ºF (180ºC). Line a large baking sheet with parchment paper or a silicone baking mat.

Place the frozen cookie balls on the prepared baking sheet, evenly spacing them about 2 inches apart. Sprinkle each with sea salt before putting into the oven, if desired. I recommend baking one sheet at a time.

Bake for 10 to 13 minutes. When you remove the cookies from the oven, they will still look doughy and that's okay; they will continue to set as they cool.

Cool on the baking sheet for 5 minutes, and then transfer to a wire rack to cool completely. Store in an airtight container at room temperature for up to a week.

ORIANA'S NOTES:

Right when the cookies come out of the oven, I like to press a couple of extra chocolate chips into the tops of the warm cookies.

EGGLESS COWBOY COOKIES

When I first heard about Cowboy Cookies, I was instantly intrigued—and a little embarrassed because I had never heard of these incredible cookies before. If you are intrigued like I was, give these Eggless Cowboy Cookies a try—they're thick and soft and full of goodness! This recipe begins with a bakery-style cookie dough and adds chocolate chips, oats, chopped pecans, and coconut flakes—something to keep everyone happy. You'll love the big, bold flavor and play of textures in this easy-to-make cookie. Be careful; these cookies are dangerously addicting, and it's hard to eat just one.

Makes 18 cookies

1-1/2 cups (210 g) all-purpose flour

1/2 teaspoon (2 g) baking powder

1/2 teaspoon (3 g) baking soda

1/2 teaspoon (2 g) salt

3/4 cup (170 g) unsalted butter, softened

1/2 cup (100 g) granulated sugar

1/2 cup (100 g) brown sugar

3 tablespoons (45 ml) milk

2 teaspoons (10 ml) pure vanilla extract

1 cup (100 g) old-fashioned rolled oats

1 cup (200 g) semisweet chocolate chips

3/4 cup (65 g) unsweetened coconut flakes

3/4 cup (93 g) pecans, chopped

Combine the flour, baking powder, baking soda, and salt in a bowl. Set aside.

Using an electric hand mixer or a stand mixer, beat the butter, granulated sugar, and brown sugar on medium speed until smooth and creamy, 3 to 4 minutes. Scrape down the sides and bottom of the bowl as needed. Add the milk and vanilla; mix until incorporated.

Reduce the speed to low and gradually beat in the flour mixture; mix until combined. Stir in the oats, chocolate chips, coconut, and pecans and mix until evenly distributed.

Scoop out 1-1/2 to 2 tablespoons of dough for each cookie. Roll each portion into a ball and place on a baking sheet or large plate. Refrigerate for at least 30 minutes or up to 2 days.

Preheat the oven to 350ºF (180ºC). Line two large baking sheets with parchment paper or silicone baking mats.

Place the chilled cookie balls on the prepared baking sheets, evenly spacing them about 2 inches apart. I recommend baking one sheet at a time.

Bake for 10 to 12 minutes, until barely golden brown around the edges, but still soft in the middle. When you remove the cookies from the oven, they will still look doughy and that's okay; they will continue to set as they cool.

Cool on the baking sheets for 5 minutes, and then transfer to wire racks to cool completely. Store in an airtight container at room temperature for up to a week.

EGGLESS CINNAMON ROLL COOKIES

We love cinnamon rolls! These thick, soft, buttery cookies include a touch of cinnamon and a sweet cream cheese icing, for all the flavors of a cinnamon roll in an epic cookie recipe! They're easy to make, taste just like cinnamon buns, and are itty-bitty adorable.

Makes 28 cookies

For the Eggless Cinnamon Roll Cookies

2-1/4 cups (319 g) all-purpose flour

2-1/4 teaspoons (9 g) baking powder

1 teaspoon (2 g) ground cinnamon

1/2 teaspoon (2 g) salt

3/4 cup (174 g) unsalted butter, softened

3/4 cup (150 g) granulated sugar

4 ounces (113 g) cream cheese, softened

2 teaspoons (10 ml) pure vanilla extract

For the Cream Cheese Frosting

4 ounces (113 g) cream cheese, softened

4 tablespoons (58 g) unsalted butter, softened

2 cups (240 g) confectioners' sugar

1 teaspoon (5 ml) pure vanilla extract

Pinch of salt

Cinnamon sugar (optional)

Make the Eggless Cinnamon Roll Cookies

Whisk the flour, baking powder, cinnamon, and salt together in a medium bowl and set aside.

Using an electric hand mixer or a stand mixer, cream the butter and sugar until light and fluffy, about 5 minutes. Add the cream cheese and vanilla and mix until well combined. Scrape down the sides and bottom of the bowl as needed.

Reduce the speed to low and gradually beat in the flour mixture; mix until evenly distributed.

Scoop out 1-1/2 to 2 tablespoons of dough for each cookie. Roll each portion into a ball and place on a baking sheet or large plate. Refrigerate for at least 1 hour or up to 2 days.

Preheat the oven to 350ºF (180ºC). Line two large baking sheets with parchment paper or silicone baking mats.

Place the chilled cookie balls on the prepared baking sheets, evenly spacing them about 2 inches apart. I recommend baking one sheet at a time.

Bake for 8 to 10 minutes, until barely golden brown around the edges. Allow to cool on the baking sheets for 5 minutes, and then transfer to a wire rack to cool completely before frosting.

Make the Cream Cheese Frosting

Beat the cream cheese and butter together on medium-high speed until creamy and no lumps remain, about 4 minutes. Add the confectioners' sugar, vanilla extract, and salt. Beat on low speed for 30 seconds, and then increase to high speed until everything is completely combined and the frosting is creamy.

Spread the frosting evenly over the cooled cookies and sprinkle with cinnamon sugar, if desired. The frosted cookies will stay fresh covered at room temperature for 2 days, or in the refrigerator for up to 1 week.

Scan with your phone for my **Easy Eggless Cinnamon Rolls Recipe**

ORIANA'S NOTES:

To make cinnamon sugar, simply mix 2 tablespoons granulated sugar with 1 teaspoon ground cinnamon, or a little more or less to taste.

BIG FAT EGGLESS RED VELVET COOKIES

These Red Velvet Cookies are soft, chewy, and amazingly delicious, loaded up with tons of melted white chocolate. Obviously, these cookies are not for the faint of heart. These are insanely decadent. Insanely delicious. And the best part? Insanely big.

Makes 6 big cookies

1-1/2 cups + 3 tablespoons (238 g) all-purpose flour

2 tablespoons (13 g) natural unsweetened cocoa powder

1-1/2 teaspoons (6 g) baking powder

1/2 teaspoon (2 g) salt

1/2 cup (115 g) unsalted butter, cold and cubed

1/3 cup + 1 tablespoon (80 g) granulated sugar

1/3 cup + 1 tablespoon (80 g) brown sugar

1 cup (200 g) white chocolate chips

1-1/2 tablespoons (22.5 ml) milk

1/2 tablespoon (7.5 g) full-fat cream cheese

1 teaspoon (5 ml) pure vanilla extract

1/2 teaspoon (2.5 ml) paste or gel red food coloring

Combine the flour, cocoa powder, baking powder, and salt in a bowl. Set aside.

Using an electric hand mixer or a stand mixer, beat the cold butter on medium speed for 30 to 45 seconds just to break it down a little. Add the granulated sugar and brown sugar and mix until just combined, 30 to 45 seconds. Scrape down the sides and bottom of the bowl as needed.

Add the white chocolate chips and mix to evenly distribute.

Reduce the speed to low and add the flour mixture; mix until it resembles coarse crumbs. Add the milk, cream cheese, vanilla, and red food coloring; mix until the dough comes together into a big ball.

Divide the dough into 6 equal portions, about 1/2 cup (125 g) each. Form rustic balls of dough and place them on a baking sheet or large plate. Freeze for at least 2 hours or up to 2 months.

Preheat the oven to 350ºF (180ºC). Line a large baking sheet with parchment paper or a silicone baking mat. Place the baking sheet in the oven to heat for 5 minutes.

Carefully remove the sheet from the oven. Place the frozen cookie balls on the hot baking sheet, evenly spacing them about 4 inches (10 cm) apart.

Bake for 13 to 15 minutes, until barely golden brown around the edges, but still soft in the middle. When you remove the cookies from the oven, they will still look doughy and that's okay; they will continue to set as they cool.

Cool on the baking sheet for 5 minutes, and then transfer to a wire rack to cool completely.

Store the cookies in an airtight container for up to 1 week. When you're ready to eat, warm your cookies in a 350ºF (180ºC) oven for 5–7 minutes or until heated through.

ORIANA'S NOTES:

If you plan to freeze the dough balls for more than 24 hours, I recommend covering them with plastic wrap to avoid freezer burn.

EGGLESS PEANUT BUTTER COOKIES

These Eggless Peanut Butter Cookies will delight kids and grown-ups alike! They're soft and chewy, with the perfect salty-sweet balance and a deliciously crumbly edge. Since my daughter is highly allergic to peanuts, I've also made these using No-Nut Butter in place of the peanut butter, and they turned out amazingly well. This cookie is a classic for a reason! Don't forget the traditional cross-hatch pattern on top.

Makes 28 cookies

1 cup (140 g) all-purpose flour

1 teaspoon (6 g) baking soda

1/2 teaspoon (2 g) baking powder

1/2 teaspoon (2 g) salt

1 cup (250 g) creamy peanut butter

1/2 cup (100 g) granulated sugar

1/2 cup (100 g) packed brown sugar

3 tablespoons (45 g) cream cheese

2 teaspoons (10 ml) pure vanilla extract

1/3 cup (80 ml) milk

Preheat the oven to 350ºF (180ºC). Line two baking sheets with parchment paper or silicone baking mats.

Whisk the flour, baking soda, baking powder, and salt together in a medium bowl. Set aside.

Using an electric hand mixer or a stand mixer, cream the peanut butter, sugars, cream cheese, and vanilla on medium speed until light and fluffy, about 5 minutes. Beat in the milk. Scrape down the sides and bottom of the bowl as needed.

Reduce the speed to low and gradually beat in the flour mixture; mix until combined.

Shape level tablespoonfuls of the dough into balls and place them 2 inches apart on the prepared baking sheets. Use a fork to make a crisscross indent on top of each cookie.

Bake, one baking sheet at a time, for 8 to 10 minutes, or until very lightly browned on the sides. The centers will look very soft. Cool on the baking sheets for 5 minutes, and then transfer to wire racks to cool completely. Store in an airtight container at room temperature for up to a week.

ORIANA'S NOTES:

For a nut-free version, replace the peanut butter with an equal amount of No-Nut Butter. You can buy No-Nut Butter on Amazon and other online retailers.

Want to add extra peanut flavor? Go for it! Fold 1/2 cup chopped peanuts or peanut butter chips into the cookie dough before rolling it into balls.

FROSTINGS

AMERICAN BUTTERCREAM

American buttercream is a timeless, fluffy combination of butter and sugar. Confectioners' sugar helps to thicken the frosting, which makes it perfect for layering high cakes. It also keeps well in high-heat situations, takes color easily, and is super easy and quick to make. However, it might be too sweet for some palates and can be a little grainy if not done right. For perfectly smooth American buttercream, follow these tips for success.

Tips for American Buttercream Success

- Make sure the butter is at room temperature before beating it.

- Whip the butter until it is light, fluffy, pale in color, and free of lumps. This might take up to 5 minutes.

- Always sift the confectioners' sugar.

- Add just 1 cup of sugar at first, and mix until smooth before adding the rest of the sugar.

- Use heavy cream instead of milk for an ultra-creamy consistency.

- Try not to overbeat the buttercream after all the ingredients have been added or you might add bubbles, which will ruin the texture of the buttercream.

- Give your buttercream a last mix by hand with a rubber spatula. It's an arm workout to mix it by hand for a couple minutes, but it makes a big difference. Be sure to really push the frosting against the side of the bowl to push out all of the trapped air.

- If the buttercream is too grainy, it may be because you need to add a bit more milk or heavy cream. I recommend adding 1 additional tablespoon at a time to make sure you don't throw off the consistency of your frosting.

- The frosting should be soft and spreadable, but not runny. If the buttercream is too thick, beat in more milk, 1 tablespoon at a time, until the desired consistency is reached. If it is too thin, add more confectioners' sugar, 1/4 cup at a time, until the desired consistency is reached.

- American buttercream can be made in advance and stored, well covered, in the refrigerator for up to 5 days or in the freezer for up to 3 months.

AMERICAN VANILLA BUTTERCREAM

Makes about 3-1/2 cups (750 g), enough to frost 12 cupcakes or fill and frost one 3-layer, 6-inch (15-cm) cake or one 2-layer, 8-inch (20-cm) cake

1 cup (230 g) unsalted butter, softened

4 cups (480 g) confectioners' sugar, sifted

2 tablespoons (30 ml) whole milk or heavy cream

2 teaspoons (10 ml) pure vanilla extract

1/4 teaspoon (1 g) salt

Using an electric hand mixer or a stand mixer on medium speed, beat the butter in a large bowl until smooth and creamy, 3 to 4 minutes.

Reduce the mixer speed to low, add 1 cup of the confectioners' sugar, and keep mixing until incorporated. Add the milk, vanilla, and salt. Once incorporated, add the remaining 3 cups confectioners' sugar; beat on low speed for 1 minute, and then increase the speed to medium-high and beat for 4 to 5 minutes until the frosting is smooth, fluffy, and spreadable, scraping down the bowl once or twice.

This vanilla buttercream can be made in advance and stored, well covered, in the refrigerator for up to 5 days or in the freezer for up to 3 months. Bring the buttercream to room temperature and mix until smooth before using.

AMERICAN CHOCOLATE BUTTERCREAM

Makes about 3-1/2 cups (750 g), enough to frost 12 cupcakes or fill and frost one 3-layer, 6-inch (15-cm) cake or one 2-layer, 8-inch (20-cm) cake

1 cup (230 g) unsalted butter, softened

3/4 cup (150 g) chocolate chips or chunks, melted

3 cups (360 g) confectioners' sugar, sifted

2 tablespoons (30 ml) whole milk or heavy cream

1 teaspoon (5 ml) pure vanilla extract

1/4 teaspoon (1 g) salt

Using an electric hand mixer or a stand mixer on medium speed, beat the butter in a large bowl until smooth and creamy, 3 to 4 minutes. Add the melted chocolate and mix until well incorporated.

Reduce the mixer speed to low, add 1 cup of the confectioners' sugar, and keep mixing until incorporated. Add the milk, vanilla, and salt. Once incorporated, add the remaining 2 cups of confectioners' sugar; beat on low speed for 1 minute, and then increase the speed to medium-high and beat for 4 to 5 minutes until the buttercream is smooth, fluffy, and spreadable, scraping down the bowl once or twice.

This chocolate buttercream can be made in advance and stored, well covered, in the refrigerator for up to 5 days or in the freezer for up to 3 months. Bring the buttercream to room temperature and mix until smooth before using.

AMERICAN WHITE CHOCOLATE BUTTERCREAM

Makes about 3-1/2 cups (750 g), enough to frost 12 cupcakes or fill and frost one 3-layer, 6-inch (15-cm) cake or one 2-layer, 8-inch (20-cm) cake

1 cup (230 g) unsalted butter, softened

4 cups (480 g) confectioners' sugar, sifted

2 tablespoons (30 ml) whole milk or heavy cream

1 teaspoon (5 ml) pure vanilla extract

1/4 teaspoon (1 g) salt

1 cup (170 g) white chocolate chips or chunks, melted and cooled

Using an electric hand mixer or a stand mixer on medium speed, beat the butter in a large bowl until smooth and creamy, 3 to 4 minutes.

Reduce the mixer speed to low, add 1 cup of the confectioners' sugar, and keep mixing until incorporated. Add the milk, vanilla, and salt. Once incorporated, add the remaining 3 cups of confectioners' sugar; beat on low speed for 1 minute, and then increase the speed to medium-high and beat for 4 to 5 minutes until the frosting is smooth, fluffy, and spreadable, scraping down the bowl once or twice.

Add the melted, cooled white chocolate and whip until smooth.

This white chocolate buttercream can be made in advance and stored, covered, in the refrigerator for up to 5 days or in the freezer for up to 3 months. Bring the frosting to room temperature and mix until smooth before using.

ORIANA'S NOTES:

To melt the white chocolate, simply place it in a microwave-safe bowl and heat in 20-second bursts, stirring between each burst, until smooth and melted. Set aside to cool.

EGGLESS SWISS MERINGUE BUTTERCREAM

Traditional Swiss meringue buttercream is made with cooked egg whites. Of course, we needed an eggless version. This Eggless Swiss Meringue Buttercream, made with aquafaba, will knock your socks off! It's ultra silky and smooth, which makes it perfect if you want a decadent and elegant finish for your cakes and cupcakes.

Tips for Eggless Swiss Meringue Buttercream Success

- Check to be sure the aquafaba (chickpea brine) has the right consistency. To do so, dip a spoon in it—it should coat the spoon, and should feel slimy. If the bean liquid appears too watery, you can reduce it on the stove top over medium-low heat until it has thickened to more of a runny egg white consistency.

- Make sure you are using a clean, grease-free metal or glass bowl.

- Beat the aquafaba until it reaches stiff peaks before adding the sugar.

- Add the sugar slowly! You can do it a teaspoon at a time or just sprinkle it in as slow as slow can be.

- The butter has to be slightly softened, but on the cooler side. I like to remove it from the refrigerator and cut it into tablespoon-sized pieces when I start whipping the aquafaba.

- Wait for each piece of butter to fully mix in before adding the next.

- After adding the butter, the buttercream might look broken or curdled, but don't worry! Keep beating and it will come together.

- If the buttercream looks too soupy, the butter was probably too soft. Refrigerate the buttercream for 15 to 20 minutes and re-whip until smooth.

- Eggless Swiss Meringue Buttercream can be made in advance and stored in a lidded container or wrapped tightly in plastic wrap at room temperature overnight in the refrigerator for 1 to 2 weeks, or in the freezer for up to 3 months.

- If you refrigerate or freeze the Eggless Swiss Meringue Buttercream, make sure to bring it to room temperature and gently mix until smooth before using. Do not overmix, or it may break.

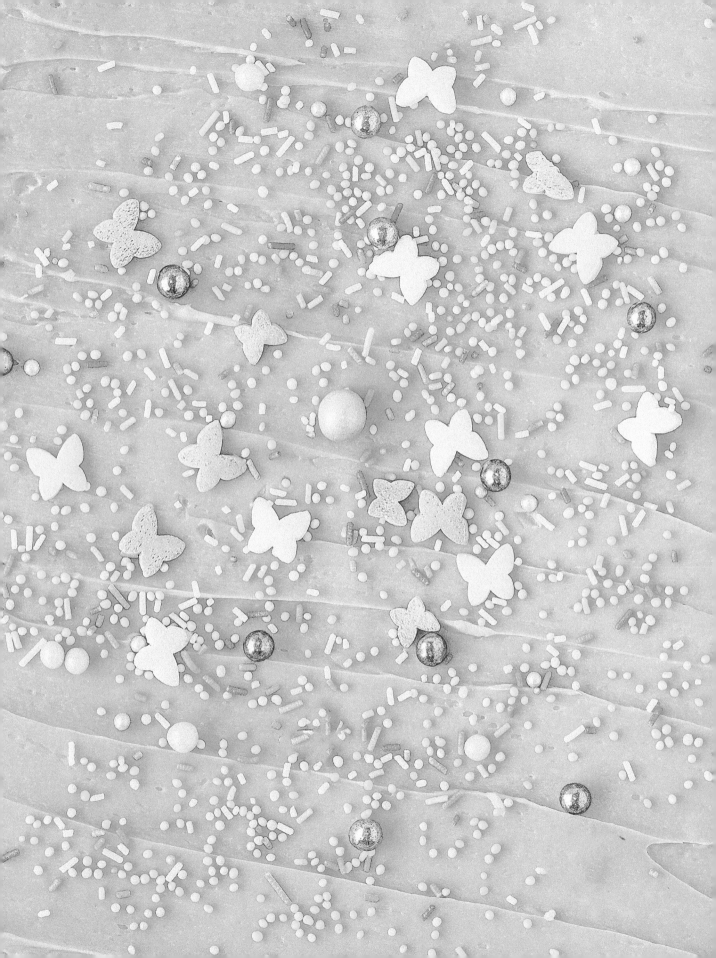

EGGLESS VANILLA SWISS MERINGUE BUTTERCREAM

Small Batch
Makes about 2 cups (500 g), enough to frost or decorate 12 cupcakes

1/3 cup + 1 tablespoon +1 teaspoon (100 ml) aquafaba (chickpea brine)

1-1/2 cups + 2 tablespoons (200 g) confectioners' sugar

2 teaspoons (10 ml) pure vanilla extract

1 cup +1 tablespoon (250 g) unsalted butter, at room temperature

Medium Batch
Makes about 4 cups (1,000 g), enough to fill, frost, and decorate one 3-layer, 6-inch (15-cm) cake

1/2 cup + 1/3 cup (200 ml) aquafaba (chickpea brine)

3-1/3 cups (400 g) confectioners' sugar

2 teaspoons (10 ml) pure vanilla extract

2 cups + 2 tablespoons (500 g) unsalted butter, at room temperature

Large Batch
Makes about 6 cups (1,500 g), enough to fill, frost, and decorate one 3-layer, 8-inch (20-cm) cake

1-1/4 cups (300 ml) aquafaba (chickpea brine)

5 cups (600 g) confectioners' sugar

1 tablespoon + 1 teaspoon (20 ml) pure vanilla extract

3-1/4 cups (750 g) unsalted butter, at room temperature

Using an electric mixer or a stand mixer with the whisk attachment, beat the aquafaba on medium-high speed until it reaches stiff peaks, 5 to 8 minutes.

Reduce the speed to medium-low and gradually add the sugar about 1 tablespoon at a time, stirring after each addition until the sugar is dissolved (15 to 20 seconds between each addition).

Stir in the vanilla extract or any other extract you'd like to use. If using food coloring, add it at this stage, too.

Add the butter a couple of tablespoons at a time, mixing until each addition is incorporated before adding the next. Turn off the mixer, and if using a stand mixer, swap out the whisk for the paddle attachment.

Turn the mixer to medium-high speed and beat until the buttercream comes together and is silky smooth, 5 to 10 minutes. Important: the buttercream might look broken or curdled, but don't worry! Keep beating and it will come together.

Eggless Swiss Meringue Buttercream can be made in advance and stored in a lidded container or wrapped tightly in plastic wrap at room temperature overnight in the refrigerator for 1 to 2 weeks, or in the freezer for up to 3 months. Bring the buttercream to room temperature and gently mix until smooth before using.

Scan with your phone to learn more about **aquafaba**

ORIANA'S NOTES:

Aquafaba is just the liquid that we usually discard from a can of chickpeas. This liquid emulates the unmistakably fluffy texture of whipped egg whites.

EGGLESS CHOCOLATE SWISS MERINGUE BUTTERCREAM

Small Batch
Makes about 2 cups (500 g), enough to frost or decorate 12 cupcakes

1/3 cup + 1 tablespoon +1 teaspoon (100 ml) aquafaba (chickpea brine)

1-1/2 cups + 2 tablespoons (200 g) confectioners' sugar

2 teaspoons (10 ml) pure vanilla extract

1 cup +1 tablespoon (250 g) unsalted butter, at room temperature

3/4 cup (150 g) chocolate chips or chunks, melted and cooled

Medium Batch
Makes about 4 cups (1,000 g), enough to fill, frost, and decorate one 3-layer, 6-inch (15-cm) cake

1/2 cup + 1/3 cup (200 ml) aquafaba (chickpea brine)

3-1/3 cups (400 g) confectioners' sugar

2 teaspoons (10 ml) pure vanilla extract

2 cups + 2 tablespoon (500 g) unsalted butter, at room temperature

1-1/2 cups (300 g) chocolate chips or chunks, melted and cooled

Large Batch
Makes: about 6 cups (1,500 g), enough to fill, frost, and decorate one 3-layer, 8-inch (20-cm) cake

1-1/4 cups (300 ml) aquafaba (chickpea brine)

5 cups (600 g) confectioners' sugar

1 tablespoon + 1 teaspoon (20 ml) pure vanilla extract

3-1/4 cups (750 g) unsalted butter, at room temperature

2-1/4 cups (450 g) chocolate chips or chunks, melted and cooled

Using an electric mixer or a stand mixer with the whisk attachment, beat the aquafaba on medium-high speed until it reaches stiff peaks, 5 to 8 minutes.

Reduce the speed to medium-low and gradually add the sugar about 1 tablespoon at a time, stirring after each addition until the sugar is dissolved (15 to 20 seconds between each addition).

Stir in the vanilla extract or any other extract you'd like to use. If using food coloring, add it at this stage, too.

Add the butter a couple of tablespoons at a time, mixing until each addition is incorporated before adding the next. Turn off the mixer, and if using a stand mixer, swap out the whisk for the paddle attachment.

Turn the mixer to medium-high speed and beat until the buttercream comes together and is silky smooth, 5 to 10 minutes. Important: the buttercream might look broken or curdled, but don't worry! Keep beating and it will come together.

Add the melted, cooled chocolate and whip until smooth.

Eggless Chocolate Swiss Meringue Buttercream can be made in advance and stored in a lidded container or wrapped tightly in plastic wrap at room temperature overnight, in the refrigerator for 1 to 2 weeks, or in the freezer for up to 3 months. Bring the buttercream to room temperature and mix until smooth before using.

Scan with your phone to learn more about **aquafaba**

> **ORIANA'S NOTES:**
>
> Aquafaba is just the liquid that we usually discard from a can of chickpeas. This liquid emulates the unmistakably fluffy texture of whipped egg whites.
>
> To melt the chocolate, simply place it in a microwave-safe bowl and heat in 20-second bursts, stirring between each burst, until smooth and melted. Set aside to cool.

EGGLESS WHITE CHOCOLATE SWISS MERINGUE BUTTERCREAM

Small Batch
Makes about 2 cups (500 g), enough to frost or decorate 12 cupcakes

1/3 cup + 1 tablespoon +1 teaspoon (100 ml) aquafaba (chickpea brine)

1-1/2 cups + 2 tablespoons (200 g) confectioners' sugar

2 teaspoons (10 ml) pure vanilla extract

1 cup +1 tablespoon (250 g) unsalted butter, at room temperature

3/4 cup (150 g) white chocolate chips or chunks, melted and cooled

Medium Batch
Makes about 4 cups (1,000 g), enough to fill, frost, and decorate one 3-layer, 6-inch (15-cm) cake

1/2 cup + 1/3 cup (200 ml) aquafaba (chickpea brine)

3-1/3 cups (400 g) confectioners' sugar

2 teaspoons (10 ml) pure vanilla extract

2 cups + 2 tablespoon (500 g) unsalted butter, at room temperature

1-1/2 cups (300 g) white chocolate chips or chunks, melted and cooled

Large Batch
Makes about 6 cups (1,500 g), enough to fill, frost, and decorate one 3-layer, 8-inch (20-cm) cake

1-1/4 cups (300 ml) aquafaba (chickpea brine)

5 cups (600 g) confectioners' sugar

1 tablespoon + 1 teaspoon (20 ml) pure vanilla extract

3-1/4 cups (750 g) unsalted butter, at room temperature

2-1/4 cups (450 g) white chocolate chips or chunks, melted and cooled

Using an electric mixer or a stand mixer with the whisk attachment, beat the aquafaba on medium-high speed until it reaches stiff peaks, 5 to 8 minutes.

Reduce the speed to medium-low and gradually add sugar about 1 tablespoon at a time, stirring after each addition until the sugar is dissolved (15 to 20 seconds between each addition).

Stir in the vanilla extract or any other extract you'd like to use. If using food coloring, add it at this stage, too.

Add the butter a couple of tablespoons at a time, mixing until each addition is incorporated before adding the next. Turn off the mixer, and if using a stand mixer, swap out the whisk for the paddle attachment.

Turn the mixer to medium-high speed and beat until the buttercream comes together and is silky smooth, 5 to 10 minutes. **Important:** the buttercream might look broken or curdled, but don't worry! Keep beating and it will come together.

Add the melted, cooled white chocolate and whip until smooth.

Eggless White Chocolate Swiss Meringue Buttercream can be made in advance and stored in a lidded container or wrapped tightly in plastic wrap at room temperature overnight, in the refrigerator for 1 to 2 weeks, or in the freezer for up to 3 months. Bring buttercream to room temperature and mix until smooth before using.

Scan with your phone to learn more about **aquafaba**

> ### ORIANA'S NOTES:
>
> **Aquafaba is just the liquid that we usually discard from a can of chickpeas. This liquid emulates the unmistakably fluffy texture of whipped egg whites.**

SALTED CARAMEL BUTTERCREAM

Makes about 3-1/2 cups (750 g), enough to frost 12 cupcakes or fill and frost one 3-layer, 6-inch (15-cm) cake or one 2-layer, 8-inch (20-cm) cake

1 cup (230 g) unsalted butter, softened

3 cups (360 g) confectioners' sugar, sifted

2 tablespoons (30 ml) whole milk or heavy cream

2 teaspoons (10 ml) pure vanilla extract

2/3 cup (160 ml) Salted Caramel (page 166)

Using an electric hand mixer or a stand mixer on medium speed, beat the butter in a large bowl until smooth and creamy, 3 to 4 minutes.

Reduce the mixer speed to low, add 1 cup of the confectioners' sugar, and keep mixing until incorporated. Add the milk and vanilla. Once incorporated, add the remaining 2 cups of confectioners' sugar; beat on low speed for 1 minute, and then increase the speed to medium-high and beat for 4 to 5 minutes until the frosting is smooth, fluffy, and spreadable, scraping down the bowl once or twice.

Add the cooled Salted Caramel and whip until smooth.

This Salted Caramel Buttercream can be made in advance and stored, covered, in the refrigerator for up to 5 days or in the freezer for up to 3 months. Bring the buttercream to room temperature and mix until smooth before using.

LEMON BUTTERCREAM

Makes about 3-1/2 cups (750 g), enough to frost 12 cupcakes or fill and frost one 3-layer, 6-inch (15-cm) cake or one 2-layer, 8-inch (20-cm) cake

1 cup (230 g) unsalted butter, softened

4 cups (480 g) confectioners' sugar, sifted

2 tablespoons (30 ml) whole milk or heavy cream

2 tablespoons (30 ml) fresh lemon juice

2 teaspoons (6 g) lemon zest

1/4 teaspoon (1 g) salt

Using an electric hand mixer or a stand mixer on medium speed, beat the butter in a large bowl until smooth and creamy, 3 to 4 minutes.

Reduce the mixer speed to low, add 1 cup of the confectioners' sugar, and keep mixing until incorporated. Add the milk, lemon juice, lemon zest, and salt. Once incorporated, add the remaining 3 cups confectioners' sugar. Beat on low speed for 1 minute, and then increase the speed to medium-high and beat for 4 to 5 minutes until the buttercream is smooth, fluffy, and spreadable, scraping down the bowl once or twice.

This Lemon Buttercream can be made in advance and stored, covered, in the refrigerator for up to 5 days. Bring the buttercream to room temperature and mix until smooth before using.

CINNAMON BUTTERCREAM

Makes about 3-1/2 cups (750 g), enough to frost 12 cupcakes or fill and frost one 3-layer, 6-inch (15-cm) cake or one 2-layer, 8-inch (20-cm) cake

1 cup (230 g) unsalted butter, softened

4 cups (480 g) confectioners' sugar, sifted

2 tablespoons (30 ml) whole milk or heavy cream

2 teaspoons (10 ml) pure vanilla extract

1 teaspoon (2 g) ground cinnamon

1/4 teaspoon (1 g) salt

Using an electric hand mixer or a stand mixer on medium speed, beat the butter in a large bowl until smooth and creamy, 3 to 4 minutes.

Reduce the mixer speed to low, add 1 cup of the confectioners' sugar, and keep mixing until incorporated. Add the milk, vanilla, cinnamon, and salt. Once incorporated, add the remaining 3 cups confectioners' sugar. Beat on low speed for 1 minute, and then increase the speed to medium-high and beat for 4 to 5 minutes until the frosting is smooth, fluffy, and spreadable, scraping down the bowl once or twice.

This Cinnamon Buttercream can be made in advance and stored, covered, in the refrigerator for up to 5 days or in the freezer for up to 3 months. Bring the buttercream to room temperature and mix until smooth before using.

BROWN SUGAR BUTTERCREAM

Makes about 3-1/2 cups (750 g), enough to frost 12 cupcakes or fill and frost one 3-layer, 6-inch (15-cm) cake or one 2-layer, 8-inch (20-cm) cake

1 cup (230 g) unsalted butter, softened

1/2 cup (100 g) brown sugar

4 cups (480 g) confectioners' sugar, sifted

2 tablespoons (30 ml) whole milk or heavy cream

2 teaspoons (10 ml) pure vanilla extract

1/4 teaspoon (1 g) salt

Using an electric hand mixer or a stand mixer on medium speed, beat the butter in a large bowl until smooth and creamy, 3 to 4 minutes.

Reduce the mixer speed to low, add the brown sugar, and beat until combined. Add 1 cup of the confectioners' sugar and keep mixing until incorporated. Add the milk, vanilla, and salt. Once incorporated, add the remaining 3 cups confectioners' sugar. Beat on low speed for 1 minute, and then increase the speed to medium-high and beat for 4 to 5 minutes until the buttercream is smooth, fluffy, and spreadable, scraping down the bowl once or twice.

This Brown Sugar Buttercream can be made in advance and stored, covered, in the refrigerator for up to 5 days. Bring the buttercream to room temperature and mix until smooth before using.

OREO BUTTERCREAM

Makes about 3-1/2 cups (750 g), enough to frost 12 cupcakes or fill and frost one 3-layer, 6-inch (15-cm) cake or one 2-layer, 8-inch (20-cm) cake

1 cup (230 g) unsalted butter, softened

4 cups (480 g) confectioners' sugar, sifted

2 tablespoons (30 ml) whole milk or heavy cream

2 teaspoons (10 ml) pure vanilla extract

1/4 teaspoon (1 g) salt

6 to 8 Oreos (66 to 88 g), finely crushed

Using an electric hand mixer or a stand mixer on medium speed, beat the butter in a large bowl until smooth and creamy, 3 to 4 minutes.

Reduce the mixer speed to low, add 1 cup of the confectioners' sugar, and keep mixing until incorporated. Add the milk, vanilla, and salt. Once incorporated, add the remaining 3 cups confectioners' sugar. Beat on low speed for 1 minute, and then increase the speed to medium-high and beat for 4 to 5 minutes until the frosting is smooth, fluffy, and spreadable, scraping down the bowl once or twice.

Add the crushed Oreos and whip until smooth.

Use the buttercream immediately. If you want to store for later use, I recommend not adding the crushed Oreos; add them only when you are ready to use the buttercream; otherwise, the cookies will lose their crunchiness.

MAPLE CINNAMON BUTTERCREAM

Makes about 3-1/2 cups (750 g), enough to frost 12 cupcakes or fill and frost one 3-layer, 6-inch (15-cm) cake or one 2-layer, 8-inch (20-cm) cake

1 cup (230 g) unsalted butter, softened

4 cups (480 g) confectioners' sugar, sifted

2 tablespoons (30 ml) whole milk or heavy cream

1 teaspoon (5 ml) pure vanilla extract

1 teaspoon (5 ml) pure maple extract

1 teaspoon (2 g) ground cinnamon

1/4 teaspoon (1 g) salt

Using an electric hand mixer or a stand mixer on medium speed, beat the butter in a large bowl until smooth and creamy, 3 to 4 minutes.

Reduce the mixer speed to low, add 1 cup of the confectioners' sugar, and keep mixing until incorporated. Add the milk, vanilla extract, maple extract, cinnamon, and salt. Once incorporated, add the remaining 3 cups confectioners' sugar. Beat on low speed for 1 minute, and then increase the speed to medium-high and beat for 4 to 5 minutes until the frosting is smooth, fluffy, and spreadable, scraping down the bowl once or twice.

This Maple Cinnamon Buttercream can be made in advance and stored, covered, in the refrigerator for up to 5 days or in the freezer for up to 3 months. Bring the buttercream to room temperature and mix until smooth before using.

ORIANA'S NOTES:

If you want your Oreo Buttercream to have a smooth texture, I recommended removing the cream between the cookies and then crushing the cookies in a food processor to form fine crumbs.

CREAM CHEESE FROSTING

Makes about 2 cups (450 g), enough to frost 12 cupcakes or one 9 x 13 inch (24 x 35 cm) sheet cake

3/4 cup (174 g) unsalted butter, softened

4 ounces (113 g) cream cheese, at room temperature

3 cups (360 g) confectioners' sugar, sifted

1 teaspoon (5 ml) pure vanilla extract

Using an electric hand mixer or a stand mixer on medium speed, beat the butter and cream cheese in a large bowl until smooth and creamy, 3 to 4 minutes.

Reduce the mixer speed to low, add 1 cup of the confectioners' sugar, and keep mixing until incorporated. Once incorporated, add the remaining 2 cups of confectioners' sugar. Beat on low speed for 1 minute, and then increase the speed to medium-high and beat for 4 to 5 minutes. Add the vanilla and continue beating until the frosting is smooth, fluffy, and spreadable, scraping down the bowl once or twice.

This Cream Cheese Frosting can be made in advance and stored, covered, in the refrigerator for up to 3 days or in the freezer for up to 1 month. Bring the frosting to room temperature and mix until smooth before using.

WHIPPED CREAM FROSTING

Makes about 6 cups (1,400 g), enough to frost, fill, and decorate one 3-layer, 6- or 7-inch (15- or 18-cm) cake

3 cups (720 ml) heavy whipping cream, chilled

6 tablespoons (54 g) confectioners' sugar

6 tablespoons (60 g) milk powder

2 teaspoons (10 ml) pure vanilla extract

Using an electric mixer or a stand mixer with the whisk attachment, whip the heavy cream on medium-high speed until it reaches medium peaks, 3 to 5 minutes.

Add the confectioners' sugar and milk powder and continue whipping until stiff peaks form, 2 to 4 minutes.

Add the vanilla extract and stir to combine.

Use immediately or cover tightly and store in the refrigerator for up to 24 hours.

ORIANA'S NOTES:

You can substitute 3 tablespoons cornstarch for the milk powder, but I highly recommend using the milk, which helps to stabilize the frosting and adds a delicious flavor.

COCONUT FROSTING

Makes about 4 cups (960 g), enough to frost 12 cupcakes or one 3-layer, 6-inch (15-cm) cake or one 2-layer, 8-inch (20-cm) cake

1-1/2 cups (345 g) unsalted butter, softened

8 ounces (227 g) cream cheese, at room temperature

6 cups (720 g) confectioners' sugar, sifted

2 teaspoons (10 ml) pure coconut extract

1/4 teaspoon (1 g) salt

Using an electric hand mixer or a stand mixer on medium speed, beat the butter and cream cheese in a large bowl until smooth and creamy, 3 to 4 minutes.

Reduce the mixer speed to low, add 1 cup of the confectioners' sugar, and keep mixing until incorporated. Once incorporated, add the remaining 5 cups of confectioners' sugar. Beat on low speed for 1 minute, and then increase the speed to medium-high and beat for 4 to 5 minutes. Add the coconut extract and salt and continue beating until the frosting is smooth, fluffy, and spreadable, scraping down the bowl once or twice.

This Coconut Frosting can be made in advance and stored, covered, in the refrigerator for up to 3 days or in the freezer for up to 1 month. Bring the frosting to room temperature and mix until smooth before using.

STRAWBERRY FROSTING

Makes 3-1/2 cups (750 g), enough to frost 12 cupcakes or fill and frost one 3-layer, 6-inch (15-cm) cake or one 2-layer, 8-inch (20-cm) cake

1 pound (450 g) fresh strawberries, washed and hulled

1 cup (230 g) unsalted butter, softened

4 cups (480 g) confectioners' sugar, sifted

2 tablespoons (30 ml) whole milk or heavy cream

1 teaspoon (5 ml) pure vanilla extract

1/8 teaspoon (0.5 g) salt

Make the Strawberry Puree

Puree the strawberries in a food processor or blender until smooth.

Transfer the strawberry puree to a saucepan or skillet. Cook over medium heat, stirring constantly, until the mixture begins to thicken and bubble, 5 to 10 minutes.

Reduce the heat to medium-low and allow the strawberry puree to simmer for 15 to 20 minutes, until reduced by half. Remove from the heat, pour into a bowl, and set aside to cool. Allow the strawberry puree to cool completely before using. Cover and store for up to 1 week in the refrigerator.

Make the Strawberry

Using an electric hand mixer or a stand mixer on medium speed, beat the butter in a large bowl until smooth and creamy, 3 to 4 minutes.

Reduce the mixer speed to low, add 1 cup of the confectioners' sugar, and keep mixing until incorporated. Add the milk, vanilla extract, and salt. Once incorporated, add the remaining 3 cups confectioners' sugar. Beat on low speed for 1 minute, and then increase the speed to medium-high and beat for 4 to 5 minutes until the frosting is smooth, fluffy, and spreadable, scraping down the bowl once or twice.

Add 1/4 cup (60 ml) of the cooled strawberry puree and mix until well incorporated.

This Strawberry Frosting can be made in advance and stored, covered, in the refrigerator for up to 5 days or in the freezer for up to 3 months. Bring the frosting to room temperature and mix until smooth before using.

> **ORIANA'S NOTES:**
>
> **The strawberry puree can be replaced with 1 cup freeze-dried strawberries powder.**

CHOCOLATE GANACHE

Makes about 1-1/2 cups (360 g)

8 ounces (227 g) chocolate, chopped
1 cup (240 ml) heavy cream

Place the chopped chocolate in a medium heatproof bowl.

Heat the cream in a small saucepan over medium heat until it begins to gently simmer. Do not let it come to a rapid boil—that's too hot! Pour the cream over the chocolate, and then let it sit for 2 to 3 minutes to gently soften the chocolate.

Mix slowly with a metal spoon or small rubber spatula until completely combined and chocolate has melted.

If using as a glaze or drip, allow to cool for 10 to 15 minutes before pouring. The ganache's temperature matters; the temperature at which you use it will determine how thick or thin your chocolate coating or drip will be.

If using as a frosting, allow to chill for 4 hours, or until almost solidified. Then beat the cooled, thickened ganache with a handheld or stand mixer fitted with a whisk attachment until light in color and texture, about 4 minutes on medium-high speed. You can use the whipped ganache to frost cupcakes or cake.

Store the ganache, well covered, at room temperature for up to 1 day or in the refrigerator for up to 2 weeks. Ganache can also be frozen for up to 3 months. Thaw in the refrigerator, and then let it stand at room temperature to thin out again.

ORIANA'S NOTES:

Always store your ganache with a piece of plastic wrap pressed against the surface to prevent any film or crust from forming.
If using white chocolate, reduce the cream to 2/3 cup (160 ml). White chocolate is softer, so you need less cream.
Dairy-Free Alternative: Use full-fat canned coconut milk in place of the heavy cream; make sure to shake up the can before opening.

CANNOLI FROSTING

Makes about 2 cups (480 g), enough to frost 12 cupcakes

1 cup (250 g) mascarpone cheese, softened

1 cup (250 g) ricotta cheese, at room temperature

2 cups (240 g) confectioners' sugar, sifted

1 teaspoon (5 ml) pure vanilla extract

1/4 teaspoon (0.5 g) ground cinnamon

Using an electric hand mixer or a stand mixer on medium-low speed, beat the mascarpone and ricotta cheese in a large bowl until just combined. Do not overmix or the mixture will break.

Reduce the mixer speed to low, add 1 cup of the confectioners' sugar, and keep mixing until incorporated. Once incorporated, add the remaining cup of confectioners' sugar. Beat on low speed for 1 minute, and then increase the speed to medium-high and beat for 2 minutes. Add the vanilla extract and cinnamon; continue beating until the frosting is smooth, fluffy, and spreadable, scraping down the bowl once or twice.

This Cannoli Frosting can be made in advance and stored, covered, in the refrigerator for up to 3 days or in the freezer for up to 1 month. Bring the frosting to room temperature and mix until smooth before using.

SALTED CARAMEL

Makes 1 cup (300 g)

1 cup (200 g) granulated sugar

4 tablespoons (60 g) unsalted butter

1/2 cup (120 ml) heavy cream

3/4 teaspoon (3 g) sea salt or kosher salt, or to taste

Heat the sugar in a medium saucepan over medium heat. Cook, stirring constantly with a wooden or high-heat-resistant silicone spoon, until the sugar is completely dissolved, 3 to 5 minutes. The sugar will form clumps and eventually melt into a brown, amber-colored liquid. Be careful not to let it burn.

Once the sugar is completely melted, remove the saucepan from the heat and stir the butter into the caramel. Keep whisking until the butter is melted and the mixture comes back together and is well combined.

Place the saucepan over low heat and very slowly drizzle in the heavy cream, stirring constantly. The mixture will rapidly bubble when the cream is added, so be careful with this step. Keep stirring until well combined.

Remove from the heat and stir in the salt. Allow to cool slightly before using. The caramel will thicken as it cools.

Cover tightly and store for up to 1 month in the refrigerator.

ORIANA'S NOTES:

Caramel solidifies in the refrigerator, so reheat in the microwave or on the stove to the desired consistency before using.

If using regular table salt, reduce the quantity to 1/2 teaspoon.

EASY SUGAR GLAZE

Makes about 1/2 cup

1 cup (120 g) confectioners' sugar, sifted
1 to 2 tablespoons (15–30 ml) milk or water
1 teaspoon vanilla extract (optional)

Place the confectioners' sugar in a medium bowl and slowly stir in the milk, 1 tablespoon at a time, and the vanilla until it reaches the desired consistency. The glaze should be smooth and pourable.

ORIANA'S NOTES:

This Easy Sugar Glaze is perfect to dip, drizzle on, or pour over your favorite baked goods and pastries. For a super-decadent glaze, use heavy cream instead of milk.

EGGLESS MARSHMALLOW CRÈME

Makes 3 cups (670 g)

1/4 cup (60 ml) aquafaba (chickpea brine)
1/8 teaspoon (1 g) cream of tartar
3/4 cup + 1 tablespoon (160 g) granulated sugar
3 tablespoons + 1 teaspoon (50 ml) water
1 teaspoon (5 ml) pure vanilla extract

Using an electric mixer or a stand mixer fitted with the whisk attachment, beat the aquafaba and cream of tartar on medium-high speed until medium peaks form, 4 to 5 minutes.

Meanwhile, combine the sugar and water in a medium saucepan. Stir to combine and dissolve the sugar. Insert a candy thermometer and place over medium heat. Simmer until the mixture reaches 240ºF (120ºC), and then remove from the heat.

Turn the mixer speed to low, and then very slowly and carefully pour the sugar syrup into the aquafaba in a thin, steady stream. Try to pour the stream right between the whisk and the sides of the bowl so the syrup doesn't get splashed by the whisk.

Once all the syrup is in, set the mixer to medium-high speed and continue whipping. The mixture will deflate at first, but then it will thicken and fluff up. Continue to whip for 8 to 10 minutes, or until the mixture is thick and glossy and the base of your mixing bowl is no longer warm. Stir in the vanilla and continue whipping until the fluff has cooled, 2 to 3 more minutes.

Use immediately or pour into an airtight container and store in the refrigerator for up to a week.

Scan with your phone to see
step-by-step photos

CONVERSIONS AND EQUIVALENTS

TEMPERATURE				VOLUME	
°F	°C	GAS MARK		US	METRIC
250	120	1/2		1 teaspoon	5 ml
300	150	2		1 tablespoon	15 ml
325	165	3		1/4 cup	60 ml
350	180	4		1/3 cup	80 ml
375	190	5		1/2 cup	120 ml
400	200	6		3/4 cup	180 ml
425	220	7		1 cup	240 ml

COMMON INGREDIENTS

FLOUR

1 cup = 140 g
1/2 cup = 70 g
1/3 cup = 47 g
1/4 cup = 35 g
1 tablespoon = 9 g

BUTTER

1 cup = 230 g
1/2 cup = 115 g
1/3 cup = 80 g
1/4 cup = 58 g
1 tablespoon = 14 g

SUGAR

1 cup = 200 g
1/2 cup = 100 g
1/3 cup = 67 g
1/4 cup = 50 g
1 tablespoon = 12 g

CONFECTIONERS' SUGAR

1 cup = 120 g
1/2 cup = 60 g
1/3 cup = 40 g
1/4 cup = 30 g
1 tablespoon = 9 g

YOGURT/SOUR CREAM

1 cup = 240 g
1/2 cup = 120 g
1/3 cup = 80 g
1/4 cup = 60 g
1 tablespoon = 15 g

COCOA

1 cup = 100 g
1/2 cup = 50 g
1/3 cup = 34 g
1/4 cup = 25 g
1 tablespoon = 8 g

CREAM CHEESE

1 block = 8 ounces = 226 g
1 tablespoon = 15 g

CHOCOLATE CHIPS

1 cup = 200 g
1/2 cup = 100 g

BAKING POWDER

1 teaspoon = 4 g
1/2 teaspoon = 2 g
1/4 teaspoon = 1 g

INDEX

Helpful links

EGGLESS BREAKFAST IDEAS

Scan with your phone to browse more recipes

EGGLESS DINNER IDEAS

Scan with your phone to browse more recipes

EGGLESS BAKING FAQ

Scan with your phone to read FAQ

ABOUT THE AUTHOR

Oriana is the recipe creator, writer, photographer, and mastermind behind Mommy's Home Cooking, an eggless food blog.

She started her eggless food blog after her youngest daughter was diagnosed with a severe egg allergy in 2013, and she refused to give up her lifelong passion for baking and cooking; she just had to find new ways to do it. To her delight, she discovered that with a little imagination and some perseverance, many dessert recipes could be made over into eggless treats without sacrificing flavor or texture.

Mommy's Home Cooking is one of the most popular eggless sites on the web. It has a devoted following among people with food allergies, intolerances, and those simply trying to live an eggless lifestyle. Oriana's mission is to prove to the world that cooking and baking without eggs don't need to be boring or difficult and to encourage her readers to grow as home cooks and learn to bake and cook eggless recipes with confidence.

Oriana lives with her family, and you can usually find her holed up at her home kitchen studio with flour on her clothes, splatters of butter in every direction, and a never-ending pile of dirty dishes. And you know what? There is truly no place she'd rather be.

For hundreds of eggless recipes and baking tips, visit MommysHomeCooking.com

facebook.com/mommyshomecooking | instagram.com/mommyshomecooking
pinterest.com/mommyhomecookin | youtube.com/mommyshomecooking